This is
Boat Handling
at Close Quarters

This is
Boat Handling
at Close Quarters

Dick Everitt and Rodger Witt

NAUTICAL

ISBN 0 7136 5840 1

Published in Great Britain 1984 by
NAUTICAL BOOKS
an imprint of A & C Black (Publishers) Ltd
35 Bedford Row
London, WC1R 4JH

Reprinted 1985 and 1987

Typeset by Orchard Repro, England
Printed in Italy

Colour work throughout the text was applied by Delius Klasing studios, Germany.

All photographs are by Dick Everitt and Rodger Witt except those on pages 33, 34 are by Cornish
Crabbers Ltd., and page 97 is by Peter Johnson. All the drawings are by Dick Everitt.

CONTENTS

The real authors of this book are the numerous skippers, coxswains and professional crew who by contributing specific examples and outlining different techniques, gave us the benefit of hard-won practical experience. More than that, they brought home to us the plain simple truth that what the boat handler needs above all is perception, patience and PRACTICE. And for that we are grateful.

D.E. & R.G.W.

A donation, from royalties, will be made to cancer research in memory of Richard Creagh-Osborne who was originally associated with this book.

What affects the boat (1)

As much an art as a science, good boat handling is more about adapting to new situations than applying a strict set of rules.

Of course, even simple boat movements demand an understanding of natural forces and the way boats behave, but the fact remains that nothing can ever replace the need for perception, or an awareness of possibilities. After all, conditions change, and a sudden wind shift, or the arrival of another boat, may thwart the best laid plan.

To add to the problems, today's busy waterways, crowded anchorages and tightly packed marinas allow little room for mistakes. Minimizing them is a fundamental aim of this book.

Here are techniques derived from numerous sources, including delivery skippers, lifeboat coxswains, and experienced yachtsmen, which not only provide insight, but underline the need for constant preparedness.

How quickly can you drop the anchor or raise the mainsail; how does your particular boat handle in astern; does she turn more tightly to port or to starboard? These are the kind of questions every boat owner must answer for himself.

He should experiment, practise, rehearse; build up a useful store of knowledge, and use it. He should also recognize that no single skipper has all the answers, and that no single solution is the only correct one at any given time.

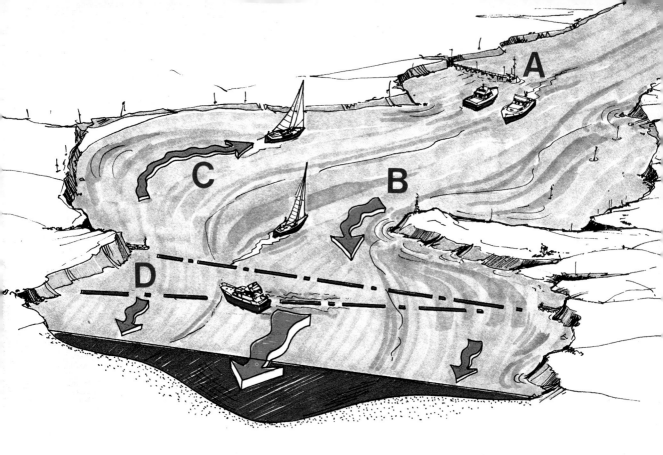

Tidal stream and current

In this book 'current', 'tidal stream' or 'tide' may be used to describe movement of water, but the principles of boat handling are the same for all.

Tidal streams and currents can speed you up, or slow you down. They can even edge you off course.

A. Always use the current as a brake, and head into it, against the flow, when coming alongside. One knot of current has about the same 'stopping' power as a Force 3 or 4 wind, while a two knot tide is as strong as a wind of Force 5 or 6.

B. Remember, currents do not always follow the channels or run in straight lines. Streams also tend to speed up round headlands, and run faster where the water is deepest . . .

C. . . . they may also push out back-eddies as they flow on their way. If you know where they are, you can use them to get back up-tide. You can also squeeze or 'sheer' the boat across the stream by allowing the flow to strike the bows at an angle.

D. With the stream at right angles to your course, the so-called 'set' must be allowed for, when homing in on a particular target.

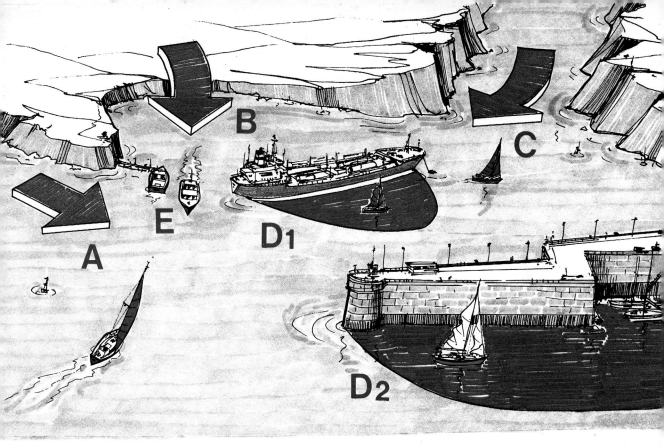

Wind

Which is stronger, the wind or the current? That's one of the first questions you should ask before starting any manoeuvre. The answer will determine your plan of campaign and angle of attack.

But where is the wind blowing from? It depends as much on local geography as the weather, and may change direction as you alter position. So study the scenery and work out what's happening and where.

A. Clear of the harbour, it blows uninterrupted, parallel with the coast.

B. But inside, it funnels round hill tops . . .

C. . . . and whistles down between cliffs.

D1, D2 There are also various 'wind shadows' thrown up by 'obstacles' like the tanker and the sea wall. They will shield you from the main force of the wind if you get in too close. In these positions you need plenty of sail high up, to catch the breeze and keep the boat moving.

E. But once you know where the wind is, you can use it as a brake by heading up into it when you anchor or come alongside.

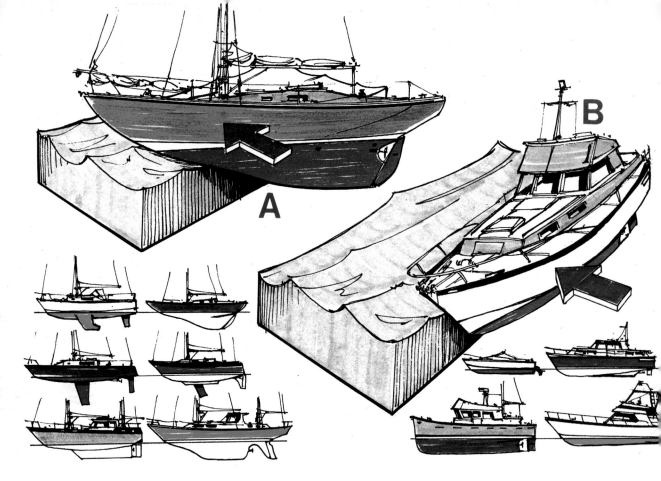

Drifting

One day your engine may fail, or your sail slides might stick. In which case it would be useful to know how your boat behaves when left to her own devices. The way she reacts depends on weight distribution, underwater shape and windage. Clearly, just a glance round your local marina will tell you that every boat is different — but as rule of thumb guide . . .

A. Most sailing boats with masts forward, and which are more cutaway at the front end of the keel, find their bows tend to blow off down-wind, and take up an angle of 30 or 40 degrees. This is sometimes referred to as 'seeking the wind with her stern'. However there are exceptions, and your boat may be one of them. So why not find out? It also makes sense to see if your can steer the boat — and what effect different rudder angles may have on her attitude. Heavy, long-keelers are

usually more docile and easy to control than lightweight skimming dishes. But much depends on basic hull balance. Indeed, some would say, better a well designed and well constructed racer, than a wallowing, unbalanced cruiser . . .

B. Motor boats, on the other hand, have a more uniform grip on the water, and are more likely to drift sideways. But again, it pays to find out!

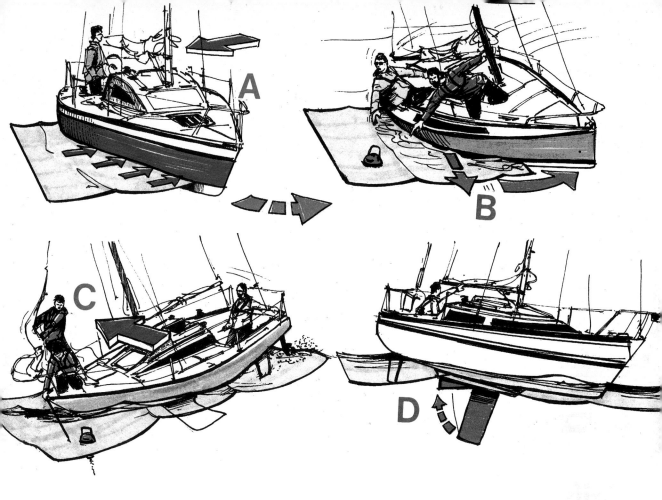

The three-dimensional shape

To get a clearer idea of what happens to your boat when she drifts, try and imagine her, not just in one plane, but three . . .

A. When moving forward some wedge-shaped hulls have an in-built tendency to slide round to windward when a side force, such as a strong wind, is applied.

B. This tendency can be exaggerated by sudden or extreme movement of crew weight. By how much, depends on the weight of the boat, and the weight of her crew!

C. Crew weight up forward can also change her shape in the water. In this case, it depresses her bow,
lifting the outboard clear. And the crew act as windage too, perhaps encouraging the boat to 'sag' downwind just at the vital moment.

D. Does she have a centreboard or retractable keel? What happens if she drifts with it up/down/ somewhere in between? You should experiment to find out. The knowledge could be more than just interesting. It might save the paint on your topsides one day . . .

Propeller effect

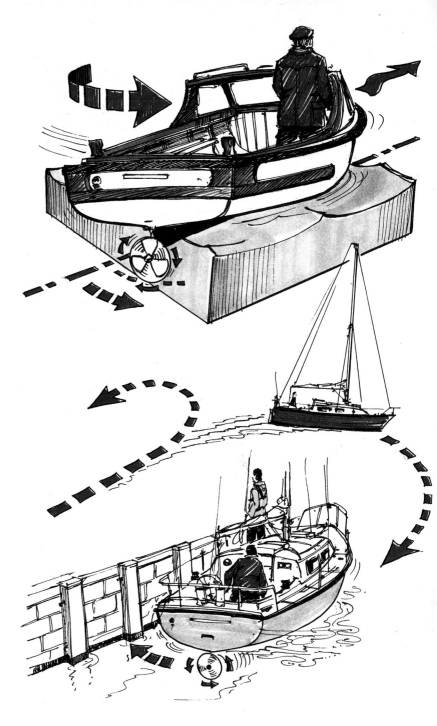

Most propellers, while 'screwing' their way forward through the water, also tend to 'paddle' sideways at the same time. Think of the propeller as a wheel rolling through the water, and it is obvious that a right handed propeller — which turns to the right in forward gear when viewed from astern — will push the stern the same way.

That means the boat will turn more tightly to port than to starboard. More noticeable at low revs with large, coarse-pitched propellers, 'prop effect' or 'paddle-wheel effect' is nearly always present to some degree, and can be useful!

For example: when coming alongside to port with a right handed prop, a kick astern will not only act as a brake, but since it reverses the rotation, will also 'paddle' the stern to port and straighten her up.

12

Twin screws

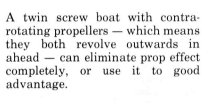

A twin screw boat with contra-rotating propellers — which means they both revolve outwards in ahead — can eliminate prop effect completely, or use it to good advantage.

For example: by running the 'outside' engine slow ahead, and the 'inside' engine half astern (to compensate for the fact that props are less efficient running 'backwards') — the boat reacts to the two opposing forces and doubled up prop effect, almost spinning on the spot.

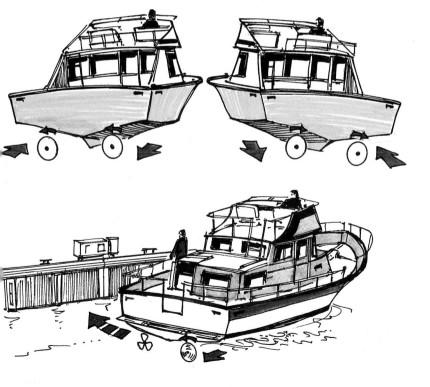

Similarly, when coming alongside with the 'inside' engine in neutral and the 'outside' engine in astern — since the rotating propeller is offset, it applies a great deal more 'leverage' and pushes her in more effectively than a single propeller could. Nevertheless, while twin screw boats are unquestionably manoeuvrable, it is a good idea to practice handling under one engine alone. Some day you may have to!

Power that turns . . .

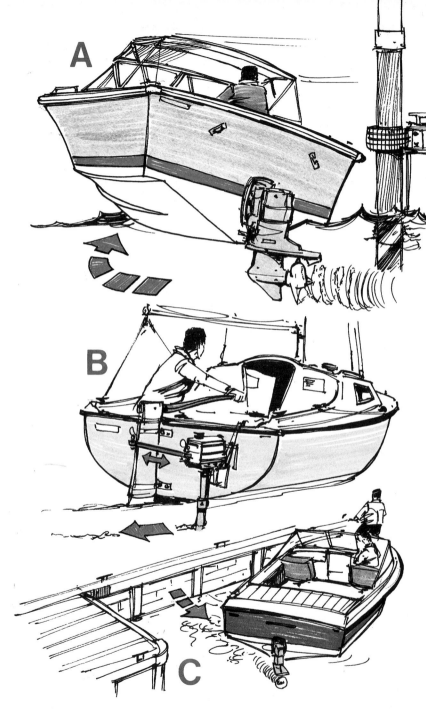

A. Since an outdrive dispenses with a rudder and turns the propeller unit instead, it needs power to steer the boat. A sudden burst with the helm hard over can kick her round at a very sharp angle, which is ideal for tight corners, but needs practice and some form of helm indicator.

B. With a linkage like this, both the outboard engine and the rudder turn when you steer on the tiller, which makes her turn tighter than by just using the rudder. The linkage should still enable the engine to tilt or slide up, for sailing or beaching.

C. While an outdrive may cause steering problems at slow speeds, it is ideal for 'pulling' your way out of tight mooring situations . . .

Basic Handling (2)

Boats move through the water and air, both of which may themselves be in motion. Their effects depend, to a large extent, on the boat's shape, size and weight. For example: the deeper the draft, the greater the lateral resistance; the lighter the displacement, the less the potential momentum.

Leaving a boat to her own devices at sea, and in different conditions, teaches how fast she drifts, at what angle to the wind, and whether or not you can steer her; tendencies you need to know, not just in the event of engine failure, but as a basis for decisive action in tight situations.

In other words, techniques must change with the boat. Deep, long-keeled yachts are generally less easy to turn than light, shallow motor boats, but, again, much depends on such things as the amount of windage and, indeed, the amount of wind.

Equally crucial, of course, is the size of engine, or engines, what kind of rig she has, and how much sail she can set. Given two big diesels, even long keeled heavyweights respond.

With that point in mind, the trend towards ever larger auxiliaries, as harbours fill up with boats, reflects an increasing dependence on power. The engine becomes a tool, providing more than straight-line propulsion. Braking moments, torque effects and side thrusts can all be used, and it pays to learn how.

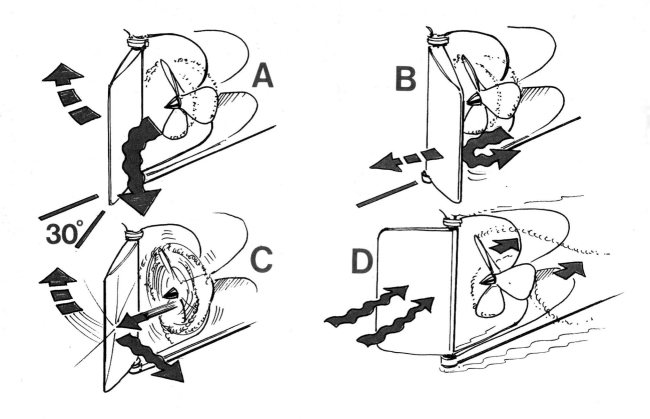

Rudder effect

A. The rudder turns the boat by deflecting water which is either thrown back by the prop, or simply displaced by the boat moving forward — which in turn drags the stern round. For maximum effect it should be angled progressively from about 15 degrees up to a maximum of about 30 degrees, because . . .

B. . . . any more than that means it acts as a brake and its turning effect drops dramatically.

C. A sudden burst ahead with a gently angled helm deflects the wash of the prop against the rudder blade, which in this case pushes the stern to port.

D. In astern, the prop wash flows forward, so the only force acting on the rudder will be as a result of backward movement through the water. So steering in astern is less positive, less immediate, and relies on momentum.

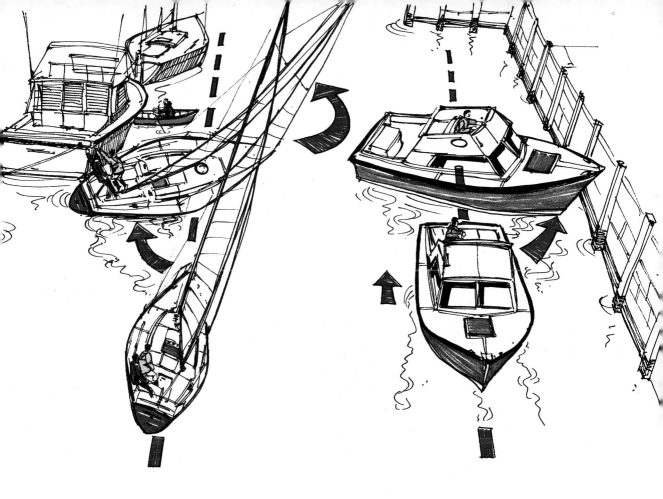

Turning — under sail and power

When you put the helm over — to avoid a sudden hazard perhaps — it is as well to remember that, unlike cars, boats have their steering at the 'back'. So allow for the fact that as the boat continues moving forward, the stern will slide round when you try to steer away. If the boat is close hauled, you should also remember to free the sheets. Otherwise she may try to luff up and sail back into trouble.

Of course, motor boats steer from the 'back' too, but the exact pivot point varies from boat to boat and situation to situation. Here, the skipper is looking over his shoulder rather than concentrating on the swing of the bow. So she motors back and collides with the quay. Sometimes, you need two pairs of eyes . . .

Moving backwards

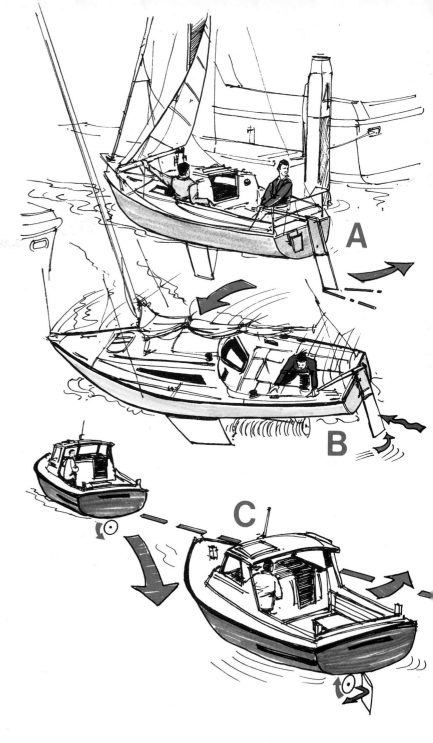

A. It is often easiest to let nature do the work. What could be simpler than holding out the sail like this and letting the wind blow you back. Naturally, this kind of tactic works best in light winds on small, light-weight boats, but large boats can do it too, especially if they have a mizzen. You should also allow for the fact that, when steering in astern, the boat will 'follow the rudder' and take a long time to react until she has built up momentum. It can help to stand and face the way you are going.

B. If you move back too fast under power, the resistance of the water may slam the blade over and throw you off course ... as well as off balance!

C. Is the prop effect kicking you slightly to one side as you motor astern? A burst ahead should straighten her ...

D. . . . though when reversing, and using forward power simply as a brake, prop effect may, of course, be less helpful, and push her stern out. In that case, you will have to counteract it with a few degrees of rudder to straighten her up.

E. On outdrive-powered craft with plenty of windage forward, it is often easier to reverse into a berth. This pulls, rather than pushes, her into position, so the hull 'follows the prop' rather like a front wheel drive car.

F. When using reverse gear as a brake, the prop effect should be allowed for. Sudden changes from full ahead to full astern may throw her sideways and drive her out of control . . . it may even damage your gearbox!

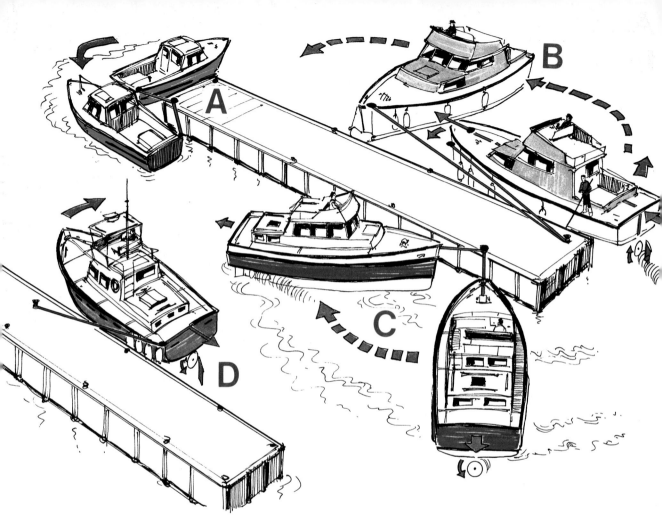

Powering against warps

A. A stern warp will hold her close to the dock under tension, so she pivots more tightly in reverse. Fend off well.

B. Powering forward with a right-handed prop, against the bow warp, makes the stern swing out. Help by pushing her clear, and remember to use plenty of fenders. Lots of padding at the bow and a couple of extra lines will be needed if you want to turn her right round.

C. Pulling back in astern against a bow warp will drive the stern in the same direction as the rotation of the prop, and needs fewer fenders.

D. Powering back against a stern spring will force her bows out.

Anchor-turning

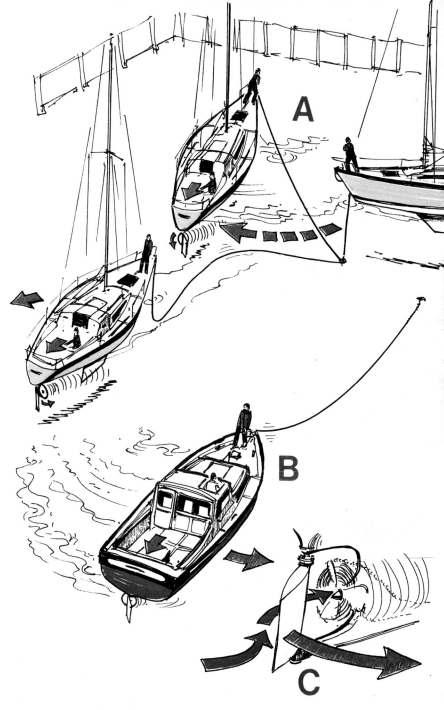

A. Dropping an anchor, with slight forward motion in neutral, allows the boat to be steered round under tension in tight corners. To stop her swinging right round, engage reverse and motor back, snubbing the cable for extra control if necessary. This technique can also be used in strong winds to stop the bows 'blowing off' downwind.

B. A taut cable (rode) is a great help particularly if, thanks to prop effect, the boat drops back off line.

C. Careful snubbing, plenty of revs, and the rudder angled in the direction you want to go, can produce a 'suction' effect which drags her over and back into line.

Moving sideways

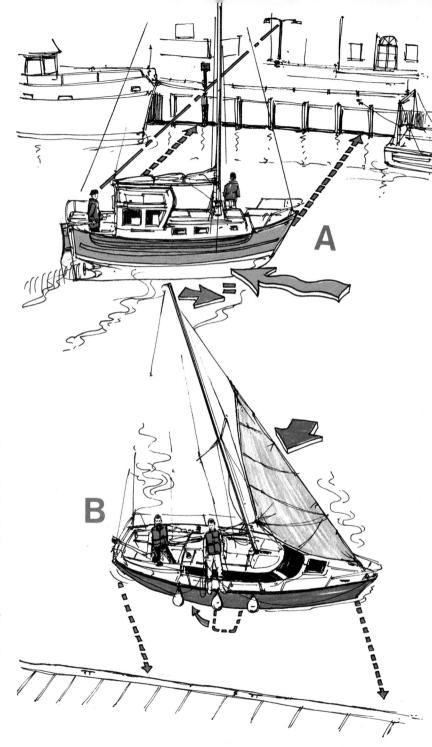

A. It is possible to 'walk' or 'sheer' the boat sideways by reducing power to hold her steady in the current; then adjust the helm so the current acts on one side of the bow and pushes you in the direction you want to go. If progress is too fast, straighten her up; if too slow, apply more helm. The faster the current runs, the more control the rudder will have. But always check your approach by lining up landmarks on shore.

B. If there is no current you can harness the wind, by simply drifting broadside under 'bare poles', if not, by hoisting some canvas. A backed jib may do the trick. If you have a centreboard or lifting keel, remember you can raise it to reduce drag, or lower it, if you want to slow down . . .

Moving sideways/ prop effect

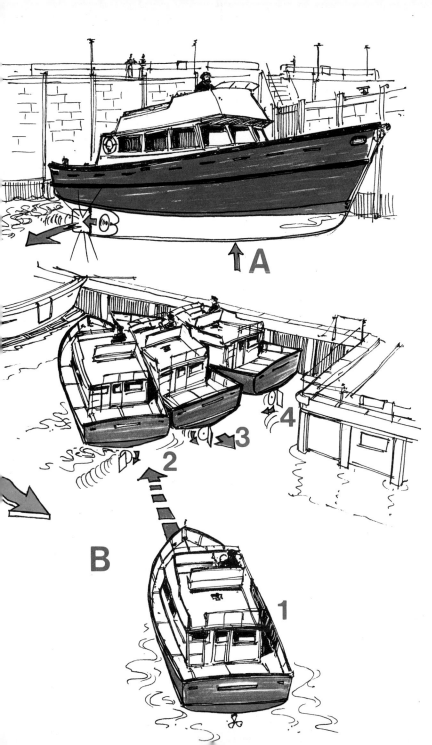

A. A burst ahead, which deflects a jet of water against the rudder, will kick her round. Used in conjunction with judicious bursts astern, this technique will help make her pivot and squeeze into position with minimal forward movement.

B. For example: at point 1. this motor boat has eased into neutral to slow down against the tide. At point 2. when almost stationary, a burst ahead with her right-hand prop effect sends a water-jet against the angled rudder kicking her over to point 3. where a touch in reverse controls the in swinging stern until she reaches point 4. A touch ahead then straightens her up against the quay.

23

Tight turns using prop effect and wind

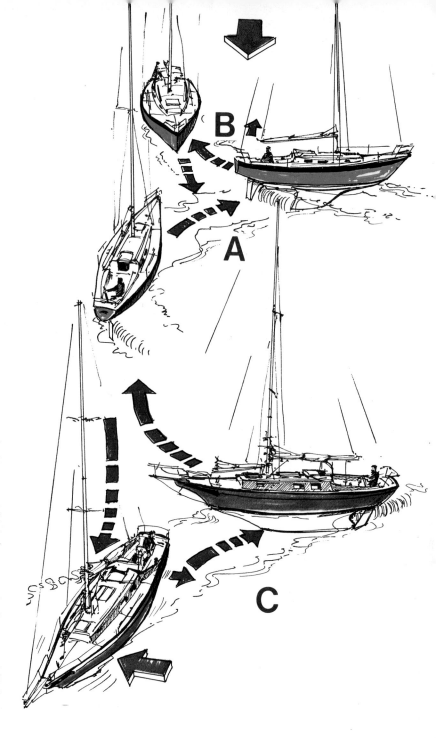

Tight turns depend on wind and current, room available, hull design and not too many people watching!

A. It is easier to turn when motoring up-wind, since the bow will tend to blow round by itself, due to the windage of the mast and rigging forward.

B. Turning can then be helped by the prop effect of powering back in astern.

C. Here, the skipper makes a tight turn in reverse. The wind pushes her bow to starboard; prop effect pushes her stern to port.

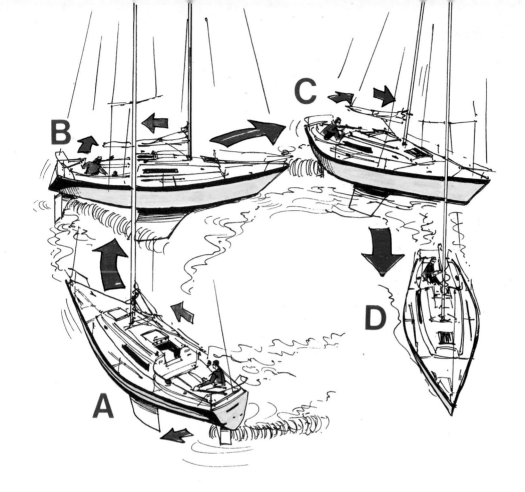

Burst-turns

Burst turns again depend on prevailing conditions as well as hull design. Some boats will just not respond.

A. With a right handed prop and the right conditions, a sharp burst of power in ahead will deflect a water-jet against the angled rudder and push the stern to port.
Let momentum take over, and slip the engine into neutral . . .

B. . . . then, with the helm in the same position, apply a burst in astern which, thanks to prop effect, kicks the stern sideways.

C. Another burst ahead, keeps her swinging.

D. Complete the turn in ahead.

Side-slipping turn

With her right-handed prop running at half-speed ahead, this motor boat starts her turn to starboard. Then with the helm in the same position, the skipper slips her into slow astern, which drives the after end to port. It is then a question of weighing up the situation and deciding whether she will continue the turn under her own momentum in neutral, or needs a short burst in astern, before completing the manoeuvre at slow ahead. The main object is to keep the boat 'spinning' and not making way either forward or astern. If in doubt, wait and see what she does, rather than piling on power or spinning the wheel madly.

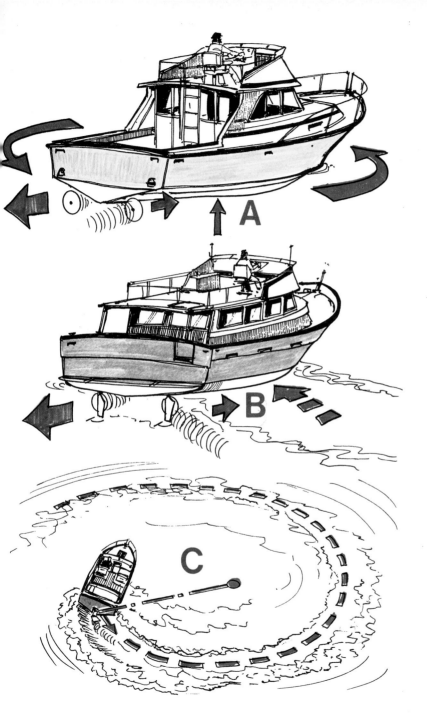

Turning with twin screws and outdrives

A. If your boat has contra-rotating, outward turning propellers, it is almost possible to spin on the spot without any help from the rudders. With the 'outside' engine at slow ahead, and the 'inside' engine at half astern — to allow for the fact that propellers are less efficient in reverse — the two opposing forces will 'twist' the boat round.

B. If, at the same time, you do in fact bring the rudder into play, you may find you can make the boat slip sideways.

C. With an outdrive, the tightness of the turn simply depends on how far round you can angle the propeller and skid the boat round.

Will she . . .

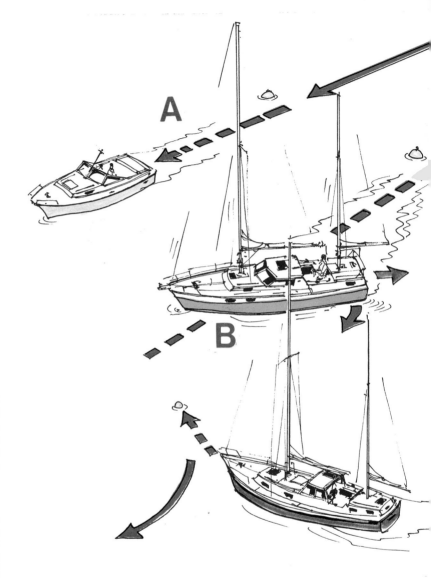

It is impossible to generalize about handling under power. You just have to go and try it out for yourself. A methodical approach is the most rewarding, but do explain to your crew why you are going round in circles all afternoon!

A. Will she carry her way, a little, or a lot? As before, try cutting the power and, by checking on buoys or moored boats, find out what she does in different conditions of wind and current.

B. Will she 'stop' easily if you suddenly slip her into reverse? How long does it take for the prop to get a grip? How much power is needed? Does the stern skid round with the prop effect? Try, try, and try again.

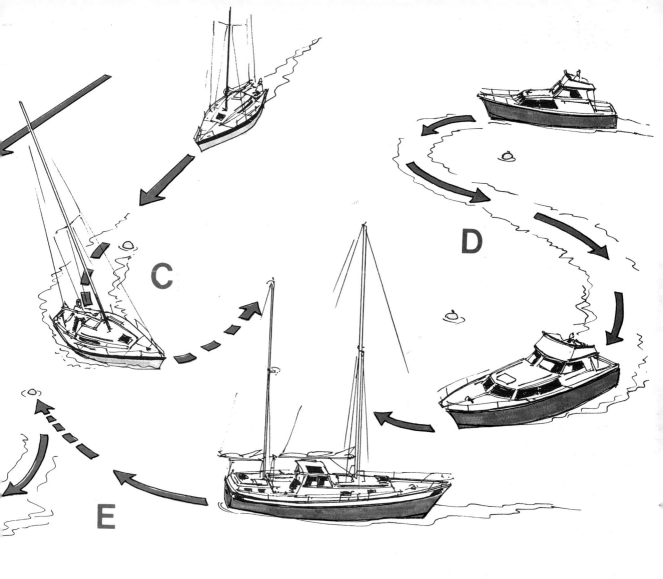

C. How tight will she turn once the power is cut? Practice with markers where there is plenty of room. She should turn tighter into the wind than away from it.

D. How tight will she turn in ahead in each direction? Does the prop effect make much difference or not? Will her windage help or hinder?

E. How tight will she turn in astern? Motor up to a buoy, then power back, first to port, then later to starboard. Again, does the prop effect make any difference? Whatever the textbooks say, remember, your boat is unique.

Will she . . .

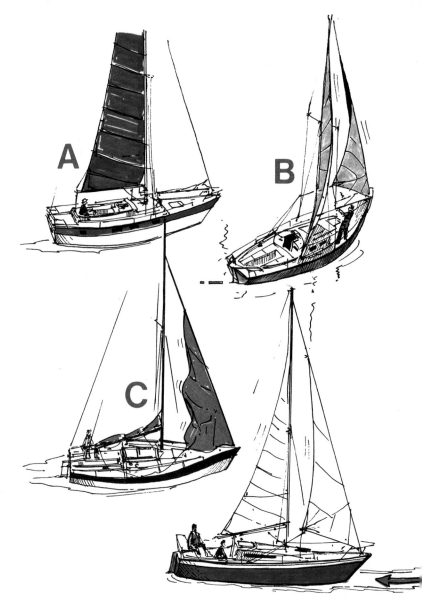

No matter how many books you read, the only way to find out how your boat handles is to find a quiet spot and practice. And try to let all the crew have a go at getting the 'feel' of her — it might be useful someday if you go overboard.

A. Some boats sail perfectly well under mainsail alone — and some don't. Why not see how your boat behaves? Ask yourself, how close will she point? Will she tack in light airs? Could I bring her alongside like this if the engine failed?

B. Will she 'stop'? Again, some boats heave-to with the jib backed, much better than others. But often, success depends on practice in different condition, so don't be afraid to experiment. Some kind of tiller-lock which holds the helm in different position will help.

C. Will she sail under headsail alone — and if so, how well? If you have headsail reefing, try using it like a throttle, winding the sail in to slow you down, and letting it out to speed up.

Try different sail combinations in different conditions. And get used to handling your boat with precision, at SLOW SPEEDS, under sail. Remember, gently does it!

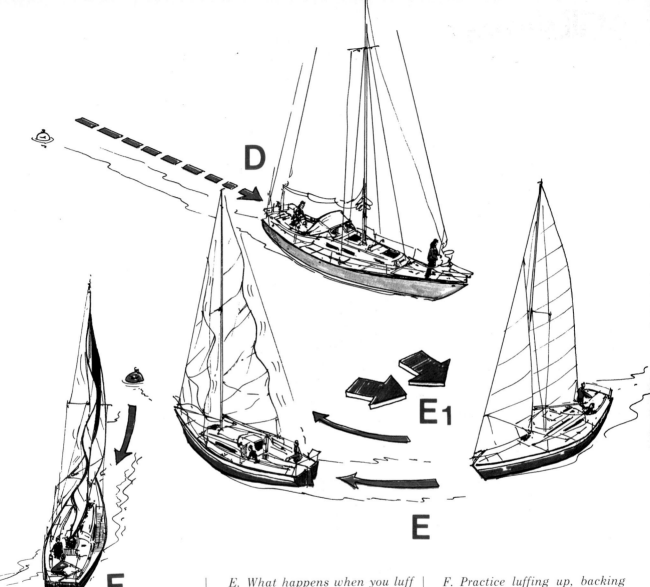

D

E₁

E

F

D. How far will she carry her way? Every so often, drop the sails, keep a check on her progress by watching buoys and moored boats — and find out. Try it in different condition.

E. What happens when you luff up? How soon will she stop? Again, practice in varying wind strengths.

E1. Remember; try not to luff up when the apparent wind direction is from the buoy because as you slow down, the apparent wind will move aft and keep her sailing — unless you ease the sheets as well.

F. Practice luffing up, backing the jib and reversing the rudder, then dropping back on the opposite tack. Will she, or won't she? It is a useful trick which may get you out of trouble, so why not have a go?

Make it easy

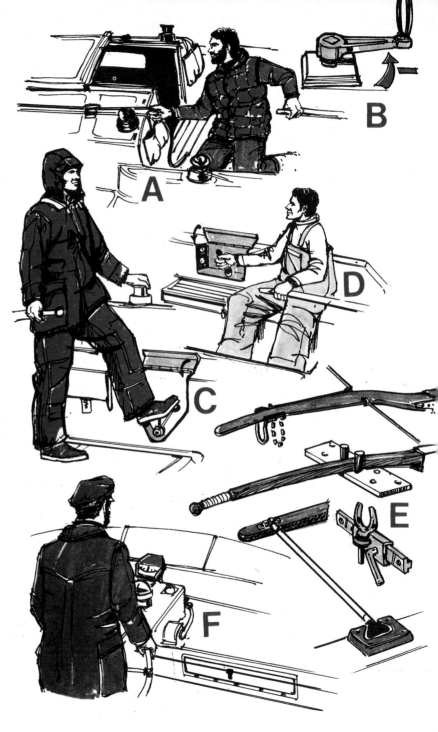

A. Don't get in a tangle! Different coloured halyards and sheets can avoid a lot of confusion. If you lead them aft for convenience, it also helps to stow the loose ends in pockets or pouches like these.

B. Which way round does it go? Stick-on arrows and labels make it easy for everyone ... including visitors and guests.

C./D. Whether you stand or sit when manoeuvring under power may depend on the visibility you have. But either way, controls should be easy to reach, either by foot or by hand. A recessed throttle is less likely to hook warps or trouser legs.

E. If you can lash the tiller, it is like having an extra pair of hands. Some people like lengths of line and jamb cleats; some prefer pin rails. Here, the holes are staggered to offer subtle adjustment. Of course, a sliding rowlock on a track allows infinite variety. Though for the ultimate in functional simplicity, a clip for the hiking stick takes some beating!

F. What is the rudder doing? Some kind of indication is necessary. It might be electronic, or, as here, just a pointer on the cable itself. As long as it works ...

Launch & Recovery (3)

Once, only dinghy sailors trailed and sailed; now, much larger craft, many of them specifically designed for the purpose, have taken to the road.

The growth in popularity of trailer-sailing is due, in part, to mooring shortages and increasing costs of storage, but another incentive is the way it opens new and varied cruising grounds.

Nevertheless, one should quickly differentiate between the owner who merely tows his boat home for the winter, with help, perhaps, from friends and a borrowed Land-Rover, and the true trailer-sailor who travels to numerous different launching sites, on a regular basis, and must be both self sufficient, and ready for numerous eventualities.

As already emphasized in Section One, a thorough knowledge of the boat involved is fundamental to all successful manoeuvres, but the key to trouble-free trailer-sailing also necessitates matching boat, trailer, and car.

Given a flush-bottomed craft with low centre of gravity; given a robust, stable, break-back trailer, with oversized winch; and given a sufficiently powerful towing vehicle with good traction and ground

This Cornish Shrimper's short mast is rigged in a strong, sensible tabernacle, which makes raising and lowering a simple operation.

clearance, almost anything is possible. Conversely, with an unstable trailer, or underpowered car, legal requirements notwithstanding, even ostensibly straightforward launching or recovery operations can be fraught with anxiety and danger.

Either way, local conditions should always be studied carefully, in advance. of course, the ideal slipway is well sheltered from waves and prevailing winds, but in real life, many are much less well protected, perhaps with the odd rocky hazard, just covered by the tide, and lying in wait alongside; one reason why inspection at Low Water as well as High Water, is always a good idea.

After the research, comes preparation of equipment and crew. Everyone must know precisely what to do, and when. Co-ordination is particularly important as the boat begins to float off, and wind and current take control.

Stern lines are needed to prevent the after end slewing round; someone should hold the bow off to stop her grating up and down on the slip; someone else should be put aboard to organize rudder, keel, and engine controls.

Whether you choose to motor or sail off depends on the depth of water, the angle of the wind, and the individual shoal-water handling characteristics of your particular boat. Naturally, these factors apply to approach techniques as well.

A simple low-slung launching trolley incorporated into the trailer, means the road wheels and bearings need never get wet. This obviously prolongs the life of the quite expensive road trailer.

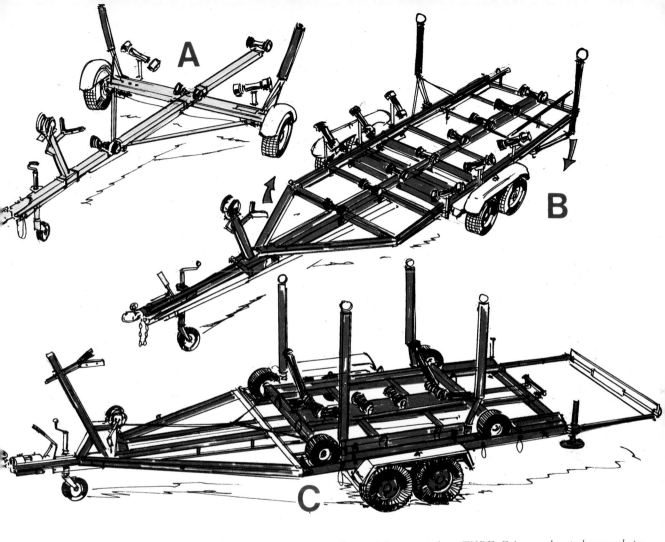

What Kind of Trailer?

TYPE A is a T-shaped trailer designed for heavy dinghies and lightweight cruisers. There is a winch-post, complete with winch, and a sliding 'jockey' wheel at the front which makes it easier to move around. It is also a good idea to fit docking arms, as they stick up out of the water and help you to line up the boat. And always make sure your 'load' conforms to the local legal requirements.

TYPE B is a four-wheeled trailer with its own brakes, and designed for heavier loads. The back half hinges down ('break-back') so the boat slides off into the water, while the wheels should stay dry.

TYPE C is a robust, heavy-duty trailer with a separate or 'piggy back' cradle which launches the boat, on small wheels with simple bearings, either down ramps or with help from a break-back arrangement. Once again, the trailer stays dry — or should do! As before, docking arms are fitted — four in this case — on which you could mark the depth to let you know if there is enough water.

35

Launching Small Cruisers

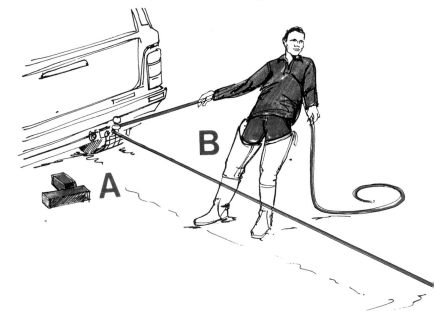

Whatever they say in the advert, it always takes twice as long as you think! Even so, do not rush it; remember, you are dealing with reasonably heavy loads which, once out of balance can be difficult to control. It also pays to let the trailer bearings cool down for at least half an hour. When hot, they tend to suck in salt water — with detrimental results. And do not forget to grease them both before and after each launch.

If possible, park the car clear of the water (in gear, with the handbrake on), have plenty of extra wheel-chocks (A) ready just in case, then ease the boat down the slip on a line (B) attached with a turn round the tow hitch. Keep a lashing (C) on, to stop the boat bouncing around on the trailer, until it has reached the necessary depth of water (marks on the docking arms help). If there is a strong current, hold her steady with a line from the stern (D), then undo the lashings and push her back, unwinding the winch as you do so. As she floats free, hold her fast on the bow warp (E), then recover the trailer.

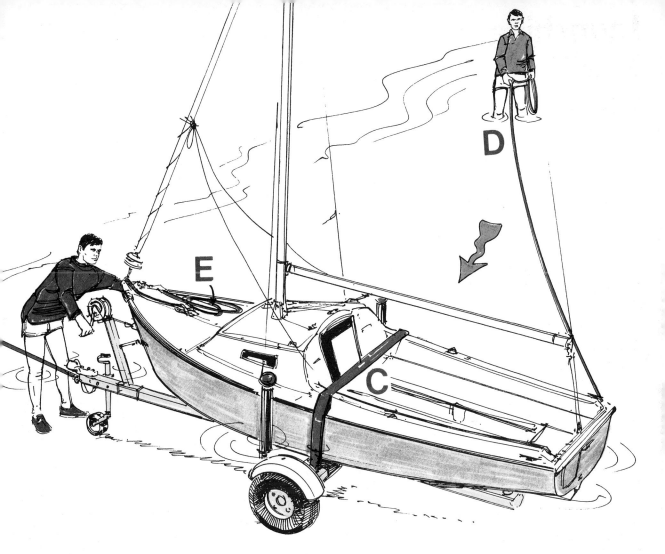

A small daysailer like this is easy to launch and recover due to it's managable size. If it's not quite straight on the trailer it can be physically moved sideways. Even so, docking arms would make that effort unecessary. And, as the road trailer is immersed it needs to be washed off and kept well greased and painted to maintain its roadworthiness.

Recovering Small Cruisers

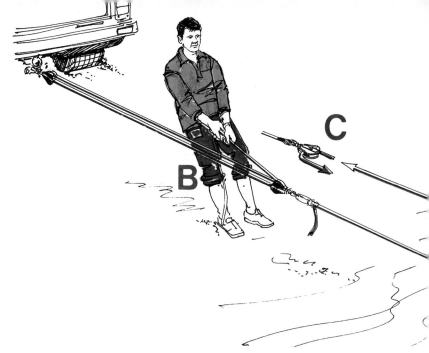

Having wheeled the trailer down to the water and submerged it to the appropriate depth as indicated on the docking arms, pass the winch rope down the middle and attach it to the boat.

As during launching, it makes sense to help line her up with a stern warp (A), to counteract current and wind — then, once she is straight, wind-in on the winch until she is positioned safely on the trailer. Engage the ratchet or brake, and lash a bow line to the winch post to make doubly sure that she cannot tip back. You can then either use the car to pull her out on a very strong line, or rig a block and tackle (B). Another alternative is to use the trailer winch, either with a line directly to the car, or via a pulley block (C) which doubles the 'mechanical advantage' and makes it less of an effort. If the trailer is painted a bright colour it shows up better underwater; you might also fit anti-chafe pads or balls to the docking arms to save scratching your topsides. Try to wash off the trailer with fresh water as soon as possible.

A

This is about the largest sized boat that can be regularly trailed and sailed by the average family. It has been especially designed for the purpose, drawing very little water and has a rig which can be easily raised or lowered. But due to its size it needs extra care in handling, as the loads involved are quite considerable. A well rehearsed launching routine is also needed to make this size of boat a practical proposition.

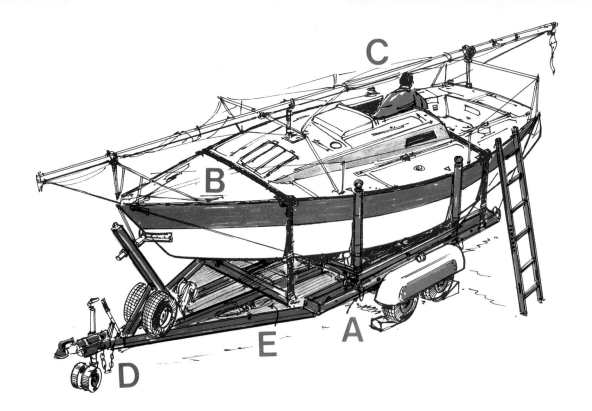

Ready for the Road

Moving larger yachts around on dry land demands greater care, and more sophisticated equipment. In fact, with a boat as big as this one, it is fair to say that trailer-sailing enters another dimension.

Gone are the makeshift lashings for example; this particular cradle is secured with proper locking pins (A) which 'bolt' it to the trailer; tough synthetic webbing straps hold the boat fast (B) — and lines from bow and stern act as a back-up system should anything break. Padding is inserted at every potential trouble spot to prevent chafe — while down below, cupboards and lockers are wedged shut, just as they would be at sea. The mast too is well padded, and supported on special crutches to stop it bending or flexing. It is also offset, to give access to the companionway and washboards (C). The trailer is a rugged break-back, with two spare wheels for extra 'insurance' — and a double jockey wheel (D) to spread the load on shingle or sand. Large mudguards which can be stood on cover the main wheels and shield the boat from stones or loose chippings, while plywood panels (E) perform a similar function on the underside of the trailer itself. Sturdy wooden chocks hold the wheels steady on slopes — and to save twisted limbs or strained ankles, there is a light alloy ladder to help you aboard.

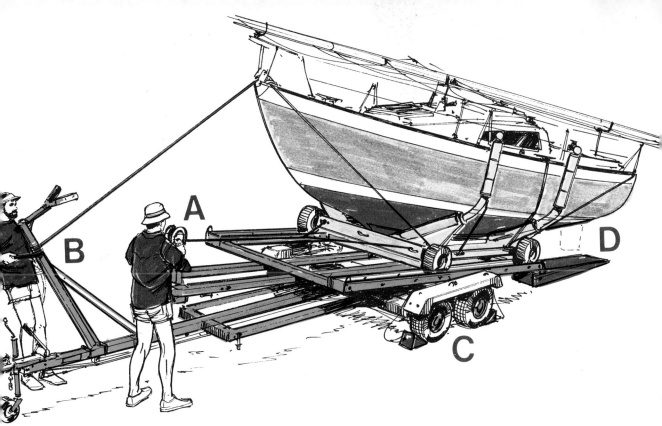

Launching Larger Yachts

With heavier boats, it is best to keep the trailer attached to the car to steady it. Once in the right position, tip the break back and, with the kind of system shown here, the boat will slide down the 'rails' on the trailer, its progress controlled by the braked winch line (A) and back-up or safety warp (B) from the bow to the winch post. Remember, the loads incurred could be considerable, so watch your fingers, make sure the wheels are well chocked (C) (some people tie them on with lanyards so they don't lose them). And be firm with young children who 'only want to help'. Make them stand well away. If your boat has a fixed rudder or overhanging stern, you may need extension ramps (D) to keep her clear and prevent 'grounding'.

The cradle can then be launched in the usual way, discarding the 'tie-down' lines when necessary. Sometimes it is best to lay an anchor well offshore from the dinghy so the boat can be pulled clear of the cradle and into deeper water. This will clear the busy slipway area for other people to launch their boats and might also save a few bumps and scratches. But remember to pack all you need in the larger boat before she is launched or you will be making several trips in the dinghy.

Recovering Larger Yachts

Clearly, the success of the operation depends to a great extent on getting the boat in the right position on the trailer. Which is why visual indications like docking arms with the draft of the boat marked on are so important.

They should also be strong and rigid, so you can make fast to them (A). In the example illustrated, the crew have lined up the arms with marks on the boat (which relate to the keel position) so they know it is safe to proceed. The boat is central, and the stub keel is hard up against a cross-member (B), which stops it slipping any further forward. There is a line to the bow, as well as the trailer, so when you haul out, everything stays together (C). As before, a steadying line (D) keeps control of the stern and keeps the boat straight.

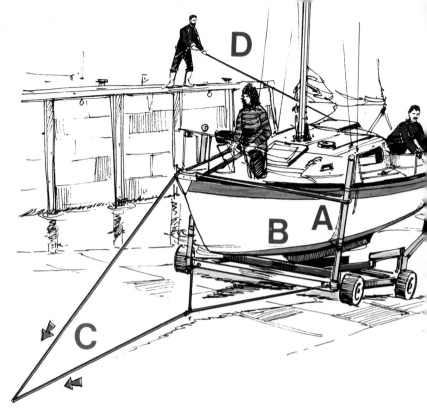

Even quite large yachts can be launched and recovered by amateurs, but usually only twice a year at 'launching' and 'laying-up' times. All the club needs is a low trolley like this and a large winch. The cranked docking arms can be swung round and pinned to accommodate different sized boats. Also the back of the trolley can be removed, once the boat is blocked up ashore, so the trolley can be pulled clear.

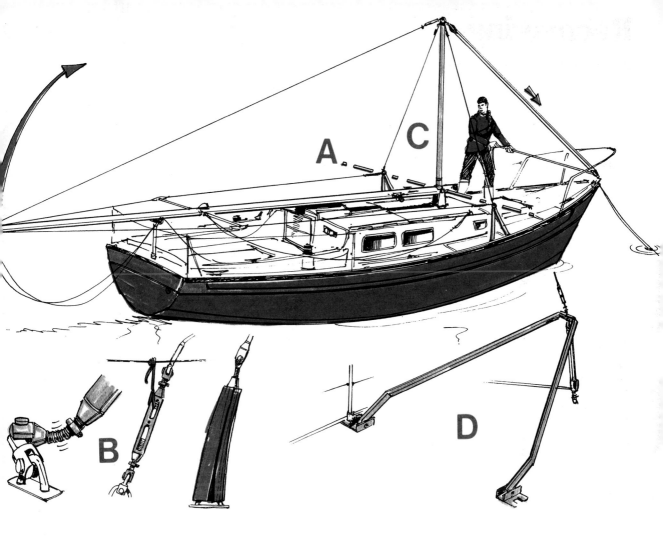

Raising the Mast

Whether you raise your mast on dry land or not depends on local conditions. Given a calm sea, it is sometimes easier afloat, than high off the ground on a trailer. Naturally, there are numerous different methods.

But whichever one you adopt, it is much safer if shrouds are attached to the boat in line with the pivot point of the mast, as they are here (A). As you can see, the chain plates are higher than normal, so the rigging stays tight as the mast arcs forward. If you have conventional chain plates, either tie the rigging screws to the guard-rails, or sleeve them with a polythene tube (B). That stops them 'cranking' over

and buckling. The lifting mechanism itself may consist simply of a rope and tackle, with a stayed spinnaker pole (C) as a lever, though some people attach the forestay to some kind of A-frame (D), which, controlled by a downhaul at the stemhead, pivots on the stanchion bases. Either way, it is advisable to raise the mast on a crutch at the after end, to make the angle of pull less acute.

Make it Easy

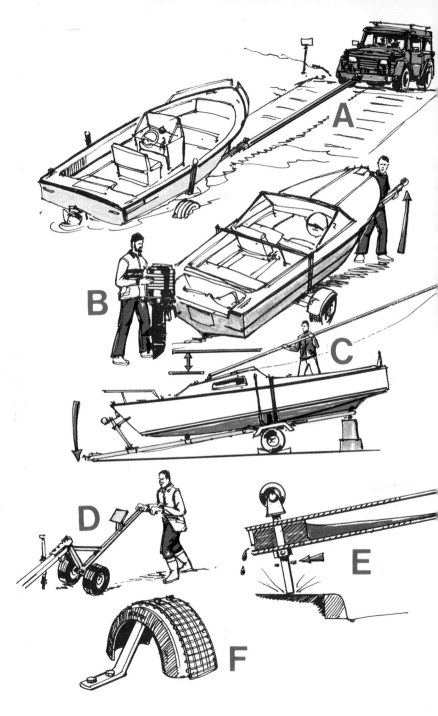

A. A front tow-hitch means you can see what you are doing. Similarly, a rigid extension between trailer and car, allows greater 'long range' control.

B. It is easier to lift a heavy outboard off the transom if you tip the boat first . . .

C. . . .the same applies when you're stepping and raising the mast.

D. Manoeuvring a large trailer is less of a back-breaking job with a 'dolly' which slots into the coupling. This one also has a pad and can carry an outboard.

E. To stop box-section trailers rusting, either seal the ends and fill them with oil, or make sure that water that gets in can get out. If you only use it for one particular boat, saw off protrusions — like this roller bracket — which, on uneven ground, may bump or scrape, or even get stuck.

F. Old tyres suitably trimmed, make excellent low-cost, anti-chafe mudguards.

Anchoring (4)

When conditions make further progress impossible, dangerous, or merely undesirable, the ability to stay put, is a highly desirable asset, which is why rehearsed and well organized anchoring techniques are good insurance against such a wide range of mishaps, from fog banks to engine failure.

But anchoring can also be viewed, more simply, as another form of mooring. It can also be used to help drag a yacht into deeper water, or as a tool to facilitate difficult manoeuvres.

Exploiting this particular facet of boat handling demands appropriate tackle, securely held in place, yet ready for action with minimum delay.

Which particular type of main (bower) anchor you choose depends, partly, on the kind of sea bottom you expect to encounter, and partly on personal preference. For example, you might compare the Fisherman with its good penetrating properties even through weed, with the Danforth which has no stock to put together, and is much lighter and easier to stow.

As far as size is concerned, it is probably true to say that anchors supplied with production cruisers tend to be the minimum acceptable, and that one should plan for extreme conditions when an anchor is the last line of defence.

The choice of cable (anchor rode) is equally important. Chain, being heavier than rope, helps the anchor get a grip, and promotes a more horizontal pull. But, naturally, excessive weight can pose problems on board. For that reason small boats often use a combination of chain and rope, usually nylon, since it stretches, thus absorbing some of the shocks as the boat tugs and snatches.

How much cable you veer depends on the depth of water, the tidal range, and prevailing weather conditions. It should be run out with some way on the boat to prevent it piling up in a heap.

In strong winds and heavy seas, you will need a great deal more cable than normal. You may even need to slide weights down to maintain the necessary curve.

With a foul bottom, a tripping-line makes sense, and there should always be a way of releasing the cable completely, if all else fails. Whatever the conditions, marking the cable in fathoms or metres, obviously makes it easier to see how much has been run out.

Most cruisers have secondary anchors, usually smaller than the bower, and used for manoeuvres such as kedging off if the yacht goes aground, though really bad weather, or restricted areas, may demand the use of two large anchors, perhaps bridled together.

But the effectiveness of this or any other anchoring system always depends of careful appraisal of local conditions, and tailoring your approach to suit.

Whatever kind of anchor you use, you obviously want it to dig itself in as firmly as possible — which will only happen if the angle of pull is close to the horizontal. That means giving it plenty of line or 'scope' (A). Under normal circumstances, you would let out a length equivalent to four times the depth of water if you were using chain, or (B) six times where the anchor line was part chain and part rope. But in bad weather where the boat may be pitching and snatching, you will inevitably need a lot more — at least ten times the depth of water!

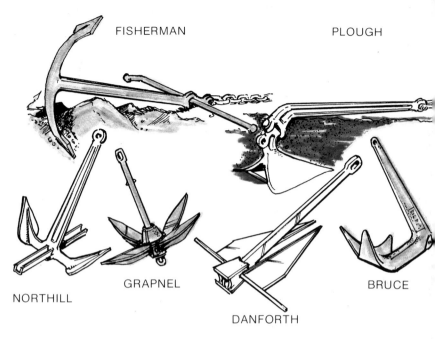

FISHERMAN

PLOUGH

NORTHILL

GRAPNEL

DANFORTH

BRUCE

BOAT L.O.A. FT.	FISHERMAN	PLOUGH	DANFORTH	NORTHILL	BRUCE	CHAIN SIZE	NYLON (multiplait)
15	10kg	5kg	5kg	5kg	5kg	1/4 in.	8mm
20	12	8	5	8	5	1/4	8/10
25	15	12	8	12	8	5/16	10
30	20	16	10	16	10	3/8	12/14
35	25	22	15	22	10	7/16	14/16

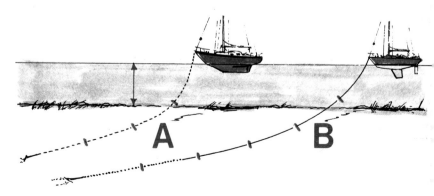

A   B

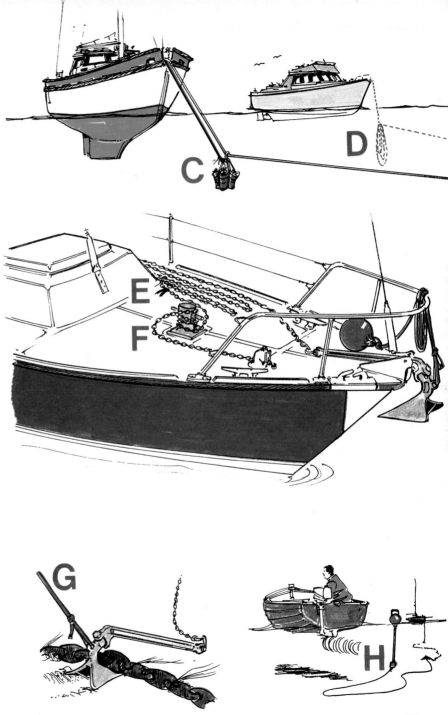

(C) The angle of pull can also be improved by lowering something heavy — either a proper anchor weight, or maybe just a bag of chain — down the line, to accentuate the curve.

(D) In tight corners, where your swinging area is limited, and the mount of line you can let out is restricted, try hanging some of the anchor chain itself, in large bights, below the bow, to act as a weight. If it drags on the bottom it will help to stop her sheering about.

As with most manoeuvres, good preparation can make all the difference. (E) Marking the links of the chain to indicate fathoms or metres makes it easier to judge how much you will need to pull out; flaking it down in lines will prevent twists and snarl-ups when you 'let go'. (F) **And do not forget to make the line fast to the bollard or cleat so the inboard end (which leads back to the chain locker) comes out on top. That prevents everything jamming under load, and makes it easier to let out more line if the situation demands.**

Before letting go the anchor, which by now should be fixed in the bow fitting, you may wish to tie a buoyed tripping-line (G) to the crown, to give you something else to pull on, should it get stuck on an underwater obstruction. You could also add a small weight (H) to this line, to keep it vertical in the water, and away from people's propellers . . .

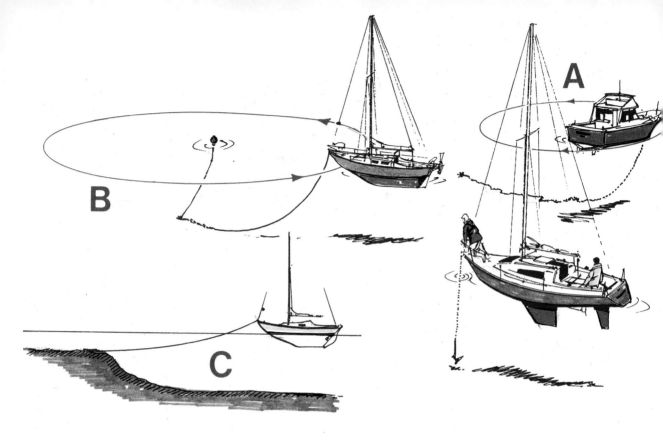

Where to drop it?

But where should you drop your anchor? Once it is dug in, will you drift back or swing round? Is there enough room? As always, look at other anchored boats, particularly boats like your own, for clues. And try to guess where their anchor is. But be careful . . .

A. . . . where boats use a lot of chain, the chain itself acts like an anchor and tends to restrict the swinging circle . . .

B. . . . on the other hand rope and chain gives the boat more scope to swing.

C. And don't be content with one sounding. Check the depth in several places, just in case the bottom shelves suddenly.

Then, having made an educated guess about your neighbours' swinging circles, let go your anchor at least two 'scopes' away from the nearest of them, just to be safe. Where there's a choice, prudent skippers anchor to leeward of the better equipped yachts, i.e. those with decent chain and hefty deck fittings — and not the ones who, for whatever reason, look a bit 'suspect'! After all, the weather may worsen, lines can chafe, and under size anchors will drag . . .

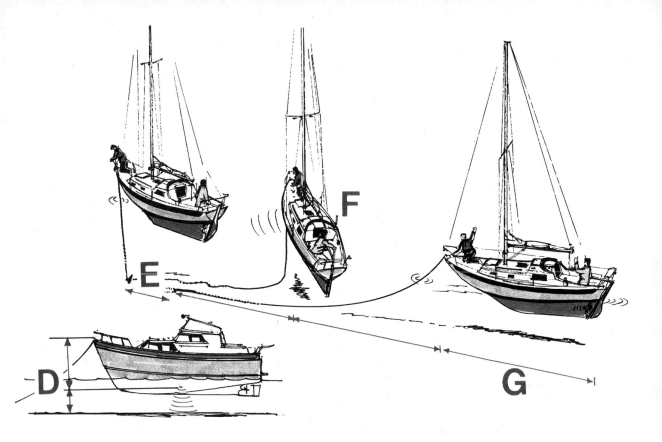

Laying the anchor

Having summed up the situation as best you can and, and allowing for the tide, prepared what you think will be enough anchor line for the final depth of water (D) (remembering to add the distance between your transducer and the height of the bow-roller), slip the engine into neutral (E). To allow for the anchor dragging before it bites, lower away slightly ahead of the chosen spot, preferably with the boat angled slightly across the current (F) which will ease you gently backwards, preventing the chain from falling in a heap. Continue to let her drift to the end of the alloted

amount of 'cable', then give a touch astern to make the anchor bite. It is useful to think of the scope you will need in terms of boat lengths (G). Where you have lots of room to swing, you might as well let out at least fifteen fathoms of chain, even if the water is shallow. It is more use to you on the sea-bed than doing nothing in the locker . . .

Unfortunately though, it is still common to see a skipper drop anchor where he wants the boat to be, and not allow for her drifting back.

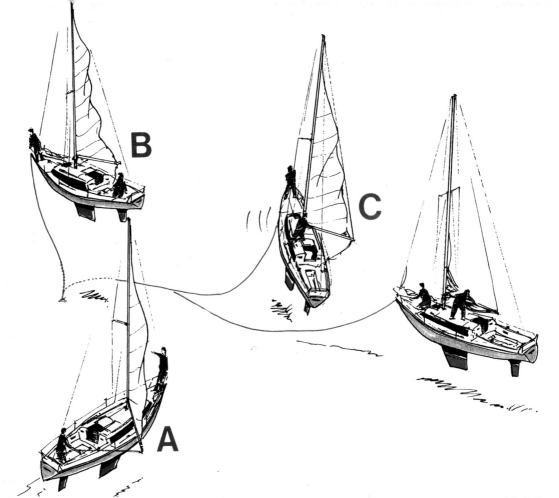

Letting go under sail

If your boat handles reasonably well under mainsail alone, that is an asset, since with no headsail to get in his way, the crew can move about more easily on the foredeck.

A. It also means you can approach the desired spot on a reach, adjusting the sheets to control your speed.

B. When you get there, luff up, and let go the anchor.

C. If she over-shoots, you want to *make sure that the cable falls to one side of the anchor, rather than directly on top of it, so sheer off at an angle. The wind will tend to drive her to one side in this way.*

So let go smartly, and ease the sheets to stop her gathering way.

With the right amount of cable out, snub it: in other words, take up the slack and jerk the cable tight to make the anchor bite.

But do not necessarily drop the mainsail until you are certain the anchor is holding. You may need to try again!

Letting go
on a run

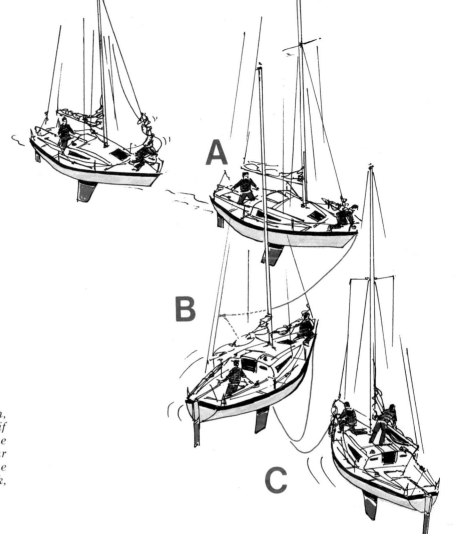

If you have to anchor on a run,
approach either under bare poles if
the wind is strong, or headsail alone
in light airs. Having judged how far
she will carry her way, hand the
headsail to clear the foredeck,
then . . .

A. . . . let go the anchor.

B. Her momentum will carry her
on until she reaches the end of her
scope. At this point she will either
round up or start yawing about,
beam-on to the current and wind.

C. With no current, it is advisable
to put the helm down so she luffs up
slightly and then pulls sharply on
the anchor, which helps make it
grip.

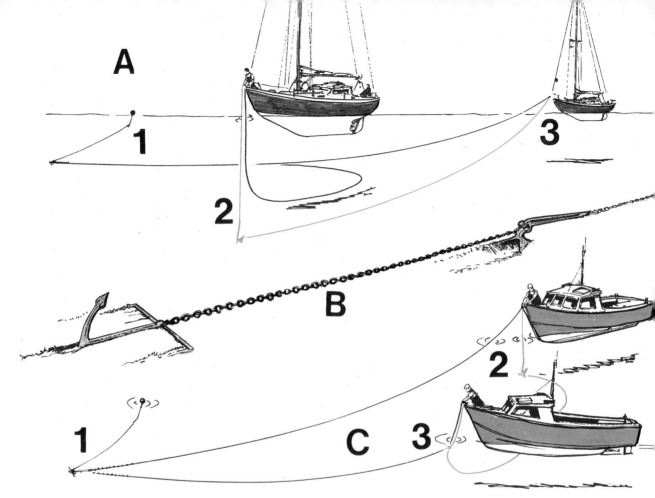

Two Anchors

A. In bad weather, or where you wish to restrict your swinging circle, it is a good idea to lay two anchors for extra security. This is known as an 'open moor' or 'open hawse', and obviously means extra work. But one day, it might be invaluable, so it is well worth practicing.

To make it easier, attach a buoyed line to the first anchor, which, not only locates it for you, but also allows you to slip the cable completely — should the situation demand.

1. Lay the first anchor as before, reversing back to 'set' it and help it dig in.

2. Now motor forward and let go anchor number two . . .

3. Gently motor back in astern, easing the first cable until the second anchor has 'set'.

B. If you can only trust one cable, anchors laid in tandem like this, can be very effective, but you must keep the adjoining chain tight. It should also be long enough — about 1½ times the depth of water — to make sure you only lift the weight of one anchor at a time when you finally decide to leave.

C. To reduce your swinging circle still more, two anchors laid 'along' the tidal flow will help.

1. Motor up-stream, lay your first anchor, and reverse back to set it. Prepare enough cable for the second anchor, then let it go (2).

3. Motor forward to a point mid-

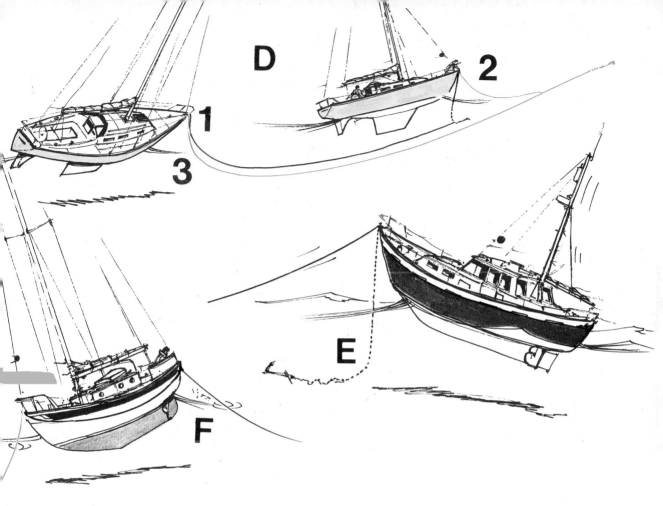

way between the two anchors, then take up the slack in the second anchor cable, and set it.

As you may imagine, the trick is avoiding tangles as you swing, but a large swivel in the system can make all the difference. Alternatively, tie the two cables together, and lower them safely beneath the boat. Either way, check the cables from time to time, and if necessary untangle them.

D. If, having laid one anchor, the weather deteriorates, you may want to lay another just to be safe. Either

pull yourself gently forward on the first cable, taking care not to 'trip' (dislodge) the anchor or, better still, motor forward at a slight angle. In this way, you should arrive at a point safely to one side of the cable. Lay the second anchor then drift back, easing the first cable if necessary, to give both anchors adequate scope.

E. If the weather makes that manoeuvre difficult, drop a second heavy anchor and chain beneath her bow to act as a drag. That prevents her sheering sideways and

snubbing the first anchor. It also eased the shock loads on the main cable.

F. In a river or restricted area, you might be required to lie to two anchors, one forward and one aft — which is fine as long as the weather stays fair. As a safety precaution though, extend the stern cable outside everything and attach it to the bow. This would be released at the stern should conditions get bad, allowing the boat to swing head to wind while still attached to two anchors at the bow.

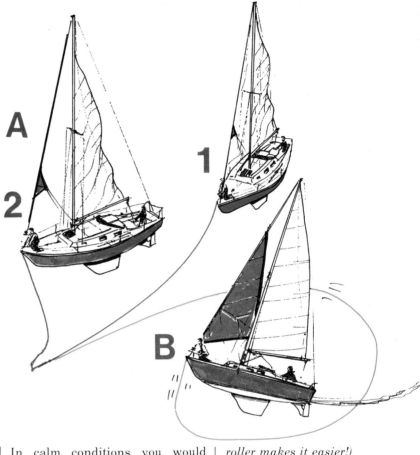

Weighing anchor

In calm conditions you would normally ease the boat up to her anchor by hauling hand-over-hand, on the cable. Once there, a positive vertical tug should dislodge it from the bottom. But given a strong wind and current, or rough, choppy water, you may have to motor forward as the crew takes in the slack.

A. Under sail, with wind and tide together, since you want to keep the foredeck clear, hoist the mainsail alone. Once the anchor is up break out the headsail, which should be backed to ease you clear on the right tack. (Obviously, a headsail on a roller makes it easier!)

With wind against tide, don't set the main; she might sail round the anchor. Instead, run down-wind under headsail alone.

B. If you find it difficult to break out the anchor (or perhaps your engine will not start) you may have to let out enough cable so you can approach under full sail, taking in the slack as you go. The idea is to reach the anchor at full speed with a tight cable. But watch your fingers! Suddenly there is a sharp tug, the boat snatches, and with luck, you are away . . .

Anchoring tips

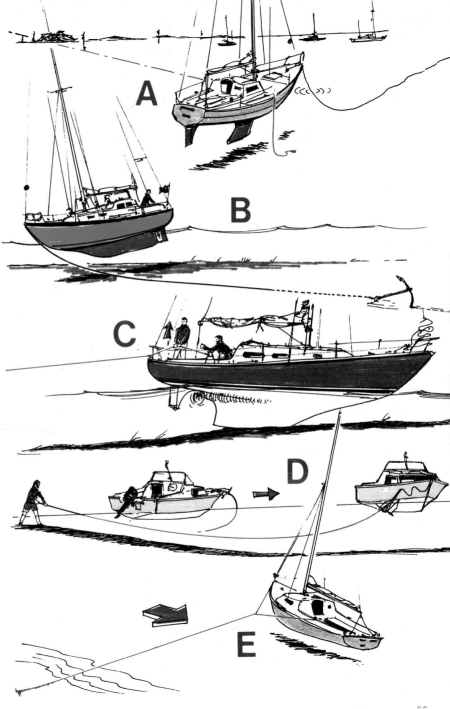

A. Is she dragging her anchor? By lining up two onshore landmarks, you can check. Or drop the leadline to the bottom, and see if it stays vertical. If it takes up an angle, you have moved!

B. If you find yourself lying beam-on to the wind at slack water, you are dragging . . .

C. To help kedge off, take the warp round a sheet winch and wind in the slack. Haul or 'swig' up vertically on the tight line and again take in the slack.

D. A trip-line can be pulled at the right moment to drop the anchor off a beach. Balance the anchor on the bow, push her off, then tug . . .

E. A bridle like this holds her steady and, in turn, helps the wind keep her clear of the beach.

Make it easy

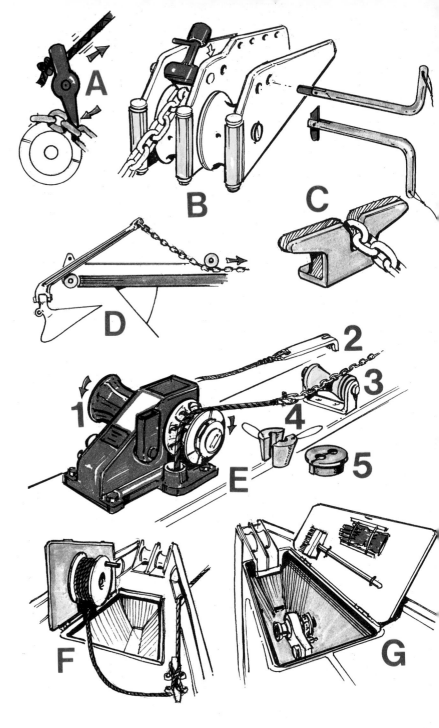

A. An anchor 'pawl' like this, tensioned by elastic or weights, notches into the chain and takes the load like a brake.

B. Good sturdy stemhead fittings are essential. This one has two larger horizontal rollers which are easy to lubricate, plus three smaller vertical ones to reduce chafe. There is a pawl to hold the chain, and a removable 'drop nose' pin to stop the chain jumping out.

C. Like a pawl, this simple snubber will also take the strain, and give the crew a rest.

D. Self-stowing anchors save your back muscles since they are ready for action.

E. An anchor winch or 'windlass' provides mechanical muscles, but . . .
  1. . . . make sure each drum, or 'gipsy' works independently, so you can use it for two anchors at once, and . . .
  2. . . . check that it has a claw which takes the load off the gears.
  3. A roller, strategically placed, will help protect your deck.
  4. Securing your chain in the locker to a line which reaches up on to the deck means you can easily extend it.
  5. A cap or bung makes the chain-pipe watertight.

F. A good place for that extra warp . . .

G. . . . or for brush and gloves to clean the mud off . . .

Tenders (5)

A well-made inflatable dinghy probably best meets the average small boat owner's often conflicting requirements for a practical tender. Inherent buoyancy and low centre of gravity make it seaworthy; lightweight and an ability to shrink, make it easy to stow on board. These advantaages, many yachtsmen believe, outweigh two obvious drawbacks: inflatables can be difficult to row in high winds, and are less durable than rigid types. On the other hand, an outboard transforms their handling, while, with care, quality models should last ten years, at least.

At the opposite end of the spectrum, traditional stem dinghies make much better rowing boats, and are drier in a chop, but few family cruisers have sufficient room to carry them on deck, and towing can be a nuisance.

A pram, in contrast, is usually much easier to accommodate. Blunt ended, its box-like proportions also mean stability with a good load-carrying capability, at the expense of a tendency to slam.

Naturally, precise characteristics depend on the individual craft in question; prams for example come in all shapes and sizes, from 'chopped-off stems' to more angular hard-chine varieties.

The start and finish of every cruise can be enriched or marred by how you handle the boat's tender. Once again practice makes perfect, so if you have time, try a few 'circuits and bumps!' All round fendering helps to protect the mother-ships's top sides, as does removing the rowlocks!

Between inflatables and conventional rigid tenders, we find numerous folding dinghies, some with articulated sides, some with fabric skins and skeletal frameworks. But often, it seems, the folding facility dominates, at the expense of a sensible, safety-conscious shape of long-term durability. Fitting in buoyancy is another problem.

As already intimated, inflatables are naturally buoyant (unless badly damaged) but other kinds of tender must use either inflatable bags, polystyrene blocks, or water-tight compartments to keep them afloat if swamped.

All tenders, apart from inflatables, should be fitted with rubbing strips to prevent damage to the parent craft when coming alongside. It also makes sense to equip them with two rowing positions, and a sculling notch or rowlock to allow flexibility under oar. Every tender should have an anchor, basic emergency equipment such as flares, and a bailer, secured on a lanyard to keep it safe even if the boat turns turtle.

Basic dinghy handling can be practised in harbour, but it pays to know how your dingy handles at sea, just as it pays to be aware of the different roles a tender can play, sometimes complementing manoeuvres made by the mother ship.

This is often the best introduction a child can have to boats and the water. On a calm, sunny day they can be 'captain' or 'crew' and actually feel how their actions affect the boat's movement. With an experienced and patient teacher they can build up their knowledge and gain confidence, which will turn them into experienced and useful crew-members of the future.

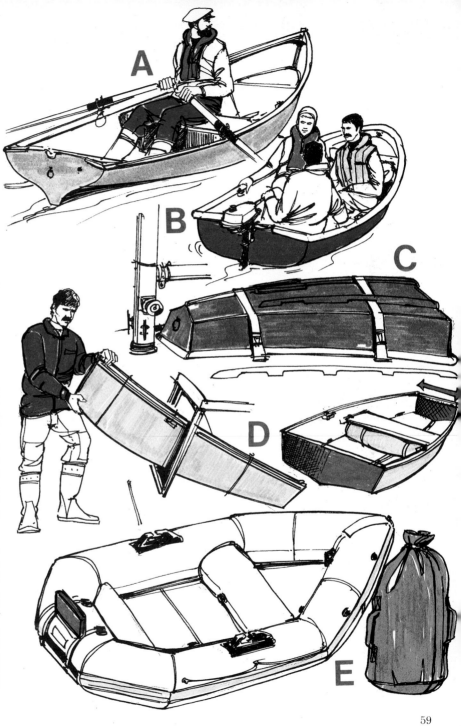

A. A good rowing boat, which tends to be 'long and narrow' with flowing lines, and perhaps even a tucked-up transom like this one, may not make a good tender, since what most owners want is a good load carrying capability within compact proportions.

B. The typical glassfibre stem dinghy probably makes more sense. It will not slide through the water so well under oar, but with its wide transom, it is better suited to outboards than other types A. Nevertheless, it is usually heavy, which is a drawback if you want to stow it on board.

C. Boxy and light, plywood prams (or praams) offer plenty of room for a given length. For that reason, there is a tendency to overload them. They can be wet in a chop, but are easier to stow than most. Bilge runners can act as extra hand holds when stowed like this.

D. Folding boats come in all shapes and sizes, and for that reason alone should be approached with some caution! Combining a seakindly, load-carrying shape within restricted dimensions is awkward enough; making it fold up as well is even more difficult. Still, where there is no room for anything else, a folding boat has its place, so long as you know its limitations.

E. Building in enough buoyancy is sometimes a problem for dinghy designers, particularly if the boat must fold or collapse in some way. Not so with inflatables. Inherently buoyant, often with a low centre of gravity, they can be 'deflated' into a kit-bag, and stowed in a locker. Not the best rowing boats (though fitting proper floorboards will help) they perform well enough and will not damage your topsides.

Rowing

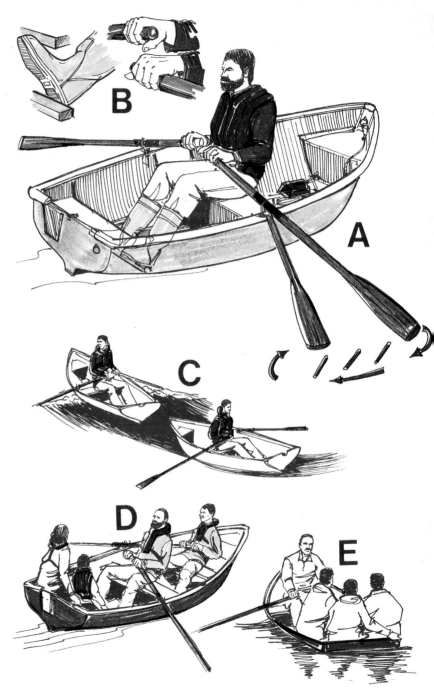

A. For maximum drive and efficiency, it is best to use oars whose individual lengths are at least 1½ times the beam of the boat, even if that means your hands will need to be staggered (one higher than the other).

B. Has your tender got a foot brace (or stretcher) to give you something to 'push' against? And is there a lip, to hook your toes under, and stop you falling backwards if you miss a stroke? Either way, you should angle the blades of the oars to help them 'knife' into the water with minimal resistance, then 'feather' or level them, to eliminate the risk of drag in choppy water.

C. When rowing through waves, pull steadily in the troughs, then pause as the crests pass beneath you.

D. Second rowing position forward means someone else can share the work. It also enables you to distribute the load more evenly.

E. Never overload a dinghy. It is tempting, but dangerous. Far safer to make two trips, than one that ends in disaster. Make sure everyone's wearing buoyancy aids, and always carry an anchor and bailer.

A. Inflatables are light, have little grip on the water, and don't build up a lot of momentum. For that reason, short, sharp strokes will help to keep her moving.

But whatever tender you have, make sure that young children are safely attached, either to an adult, or if the boat is fully buoyant, to the dinghy itself. It is also a good idea to ask a forward-facing crew member to direct you. It saves having to keep turning round!

B. Most inflatable have fairly secure rowlocks — some even have locking devices — but if you should lose an oar, try paddling over the bow.

C. If you lose or break a rowlock a rope strop like this will probably get you home.

D. If you lose an oar on a rigid dinghy, it is easiest to paddle from the stern quarter, since the heeled shape makes it easier to control. Push out and away at the end of each stroke to help keep her straight.

E. The traditional means of propulsion with one oar, is sculling. Some people do it standing up, other prefer kneeling down, but . . .

F. . . . it always requires practice! Remember to keep your wrist beneath the oar, and turn the blade at the end of each stroke, so it cuts backwards and forwards at an angle of about 40 degrees, with the leading edge always pointing towards the boat.

G. You can even scull over the bow, which means you can see where you are going. Surprisingly perhaps, some sailing dinghies scull better this way, but stern-first!

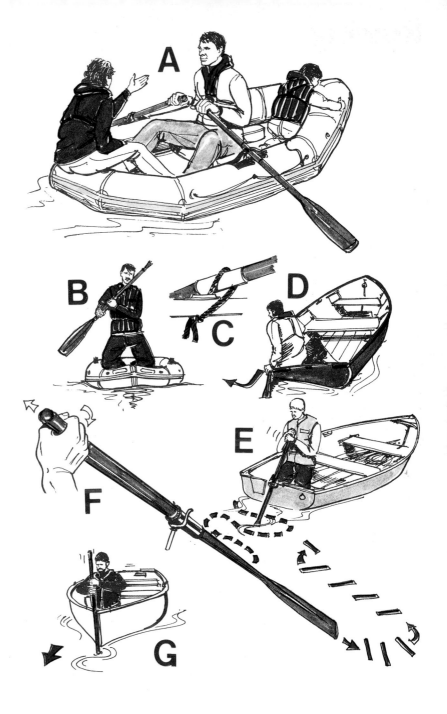

Rowing out and back

A1. When coming alongside a quay, start to turn gently upstream, either by pulling harder on what will eventually be the nearside oar — or simply drag the offside oar.

A2. For a 'quick spin', either dip the offside oar, or push the oars in different directions.

A3. As you reach your destination, unship the nearside oar, using the other one to hold her steady.

When rowing out to the mother ship, aim well up-stream (B1), and ease your way across the current at an angle (B2).

B3. Unship the inboard oar, at about this angle, as you feel the tide pushing you in alongside.

Traditionally, oars should if possible be stowed blade forward to keep passengers in the stern dry!

Laying a kedge

Unlike many manoeuvres, this one is often necessitated by sudden unforeseen circumstances — like a particularly awkward berth from which you must bail yourself out, or running aground — and, not surprisingly, skippers may be tempted to rush it. That in turn increases the risk of an accident, so work out a simple check-list in advance. Do not forget to wear a buoyancy aid and, if possible, take another crew member with you.

First, place the heavy kedge in the dinghy (with a small amount of chain) before climbing aboard yourself. Ideally, attach the kedge over the transom with a piece of light line which you can unhitch from the centre thwart, although normally you only have time to stow it separately in the dinghy. Then flake down the warp. Start at the transom, so it pays out gently, a bit at a time. That's better than paying out the line from the mother ship and towing a long unwieldy loop across the tide.

Work out how much warp you will need, then add a good 50 feet (A) to get you well past the point where the anchor should be dropped; apart from anything else, it allows the crew back on the yacht to haul away to make the anchor dig in, without losing ground.

As always, study the effects of the tide. In a strong current, you may have to row well up stream, to avoid being swept past the spot you were aiming for.

Dinghy with outboard

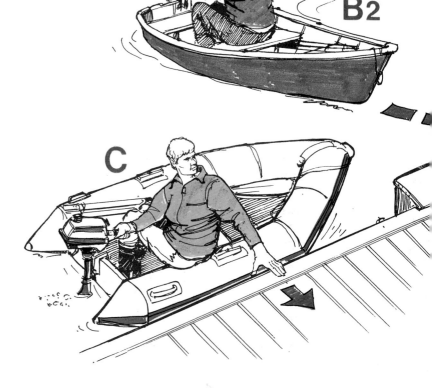

In strong winds or currents, or when your tender is carrying heavy loads perhaps over long distances, to a mother ship offshore, a small, reliable outboard saves your muscles, is more convenient, and may be a positive safety factor.

But, of course, unless you keep it well maintained, it is unreasonable to expect it to start 'first pull' every time! Prudent skippers also carry at least one spare spark plug along with the necessary spanner, and pliers. And remember, you should still carry oars, a bailer, and an anchor, just in case it breaks down . . .

A. Few small outboards are fitted with a clutch, or any kind of 'neutral' device, so when coming alongside, get used to knowing how far the boat will 'carry' in different conditions once the engine is stopped. With practice, it may be possible to switch off the fuel supply at precisely the right moment, but be warned: small outboards run much longer than you might expect, even when restricted to what it left in the carburettor.

A1. The final approach, as you drift in under momentum alone, can be ruined if you upset the trim. So make sure the crew stays put!

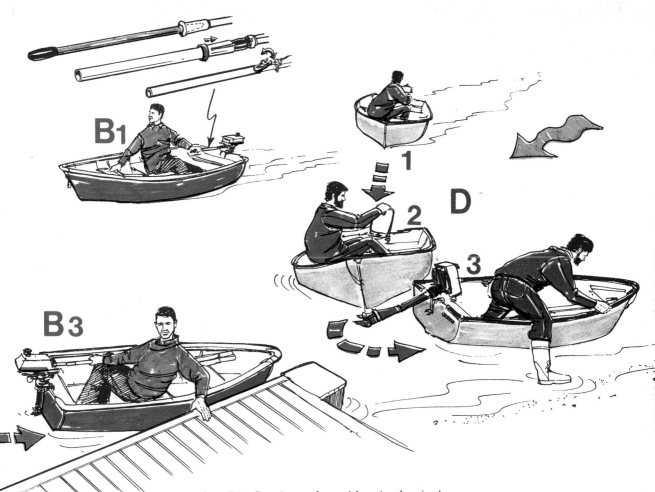

B1. Trim is always important, never more so than when manoeuvring singlehanded, when the tendency is to sit aft and depress the transom. Try and sit amidships, either by using a tiller extension (a plastic pipe or a stick with a fork in it can sometimes be used to operate the throttle) — or by making improvised side seats, perhaps with the oars.

B2. Coming alongside single-handed is much the same as before. Either stop the engine, or turn off the fuel, and swing her up-tide so she drifts gently against the quay . . .

B3. . . . as you fend off with your free hand.

C. With no clutch (or neutral) the temptation is to cast off, then try and start the engine. But it is wiser to let the engine warm up while the boat is still attached to the dock, before slipping the line and pushing her out, or if necessary row her clear.

D1. When approaching a beach, cut the fuel early (or get closer and press the 'stop' button) then let her carry her way across the current . . .

D2. . . . before tilting the engine, once it is no longer running . . .

D3. . . . and moving your body weight to slew the boat round. That prevents the bow from juddering to a halt on the bottom — which may damage the gel coat. Also you can get ashore without water going over your boot tops!

Make it easy for yourself

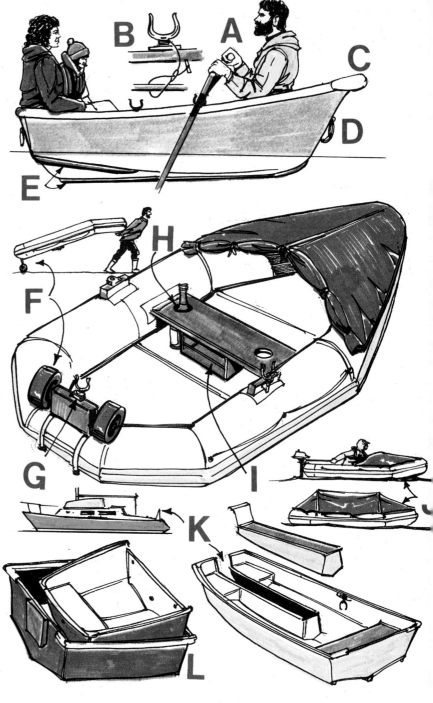

A. A second rowing position makes it easier to trim the boat out level.

B. Rowlocks should be secured with a lanyard round the neck (not through the hole at the bottom), so you cannot lose them over the side.

C. The bow can be a 'battering ram'. Protect it with a large padded fender, and the mother ship will be safer too.

D. Unlike a rigid U-bolt, a bow-ring like this folds down out of the way, so there's less chance of it doing any damage.

E. Rubbing-bands, will protect her bottom when you beach her.

F. With wheels like these, you can trundle her up (or down) the beach like a wheelbarrow.

G. Want to try sculling? A rowlock will make it possible. It can also act as a fairlead for the kedge warp.

H. Do not forget the drink; it needs special care! Tailor-made stowage holes will keep it secure.

I. Where to keep tools and odds and ends? A box like this is ideal.

J. Spray dodgers are almost essential on outboard-powered inflatables, if you want your stores to stay dry. They can even help turn your dinghy into a makeshift liferaft.

K. This dinghy has a removable section, and stows around the mast . . .

L. . . . this one comes apart, so one half fits inside the other!

Picking up and letting go (6)

As already shown, wind and current can slow you down, or speed you up. Analyzing these effects is crucial to successful handling, particularly when picking up moorings. Here, it makes sense to determine the best line of approach long before reaching the pick-up point. That in itself, unless wind and current are running in the same direction, many entail a certain amount of experiment.

Which force will you use as a brake? Is the current stronger than the wind, or vice versa. Normally, under sail, you would stop head to wind, but it could be that a fierce current flowing in the direction you want to go, makes that a dangerous manoeuvre. Instead, it might be better to reach, or run up under foresail alone; with reefing gear, you could actually reduce headsail area progressively, as you do so. It all depends on your boat, her rig, and prevailing conditions.

In any case, the skipper should work out his plan of attack carefully, with some idea of an escape route if things go wrong, then give clear, precise instructions to everyone involved, and proceed in a calm and positive manner.

A self-closing hook makes single handed mooring easier. If it is attached to a strop, which slides on a fore and aft line the boat will not drift too far back.

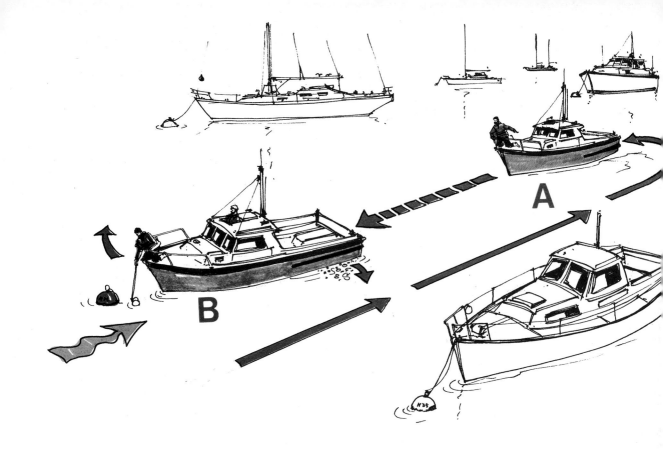

Picking up a mooring

A. Which has the greater effect, the tide or the wind? It depends, to some extent, on the kind of boat you have. So look at similar shaped craft on single buoy moorings and note which direction they lie in. That will tell you the best angle of approach. But do not attempt it until you have motored up to the buoy and seen how much room you have to manoeuvre. Then try her on the correct line, and experiment with the throttle. When you finally decide to 'move in', have the crew on the foredeck. He can tell you, with a simple system of prearranged signals whether your approach is too fast or too slow. If it is too fast, ease the throttle, or slip her into neutral.

B. In extreme cases, a few gentle revs in astern may be needed. But avoid sudden bursts of power, which might kick her stern over and push you off course.

Keep her under control all the way in. If you are too timid, the wind may catch her bow and ruin your chances.

A. Some skippers prefer to 'come alongside' the buoy, keeping it in view all the while, rather than aiming straight for it. This method also means that the crew picks up the buoy from a point where the freeboard is lower, without having to reach through the pulpit. But make sure the boat is as still as possible while he (or, indeed she) takes the buoy to the bow. If the boat is still moving too much, it may be safer to drop the buoy and go round again. Better that than torn muscles or a crew in the water!

B. If you are singlehanded, a reliable auto-pilot may be set to steer the boat while you go and pick up the buoy yourself. But first slow the boat down so she is only just moving forward . . .

C. Auto pilots with remote course adjusters allow you to steer the boat from the bow. Even easier!

If not blessed with an auto-pilot, rig a long bow line with a snap-hook, and attach it when the buoy comes within reach of the cockpit. Then haul in quickly so you do not drop back and foul other boats.

Picking up a mooring under sail

This manoeuvre can be one of the simplest, or one of the hardest; it all depends . . .

A. Given plenty of room, not too much tide, and a well-balanced boat, you approach on a broad reach, under mainsail alone, regulating boat speed by adjusting the sheet. As you let it out, the boat slows down, as you pull it in, she speeds up. Ease it right off just before you luff for the buoy, and the sail feathers, bringing the boat to a standstill. Of course, life is not always like that, but suffice it to say, with room to manoeuvre, you can always go round again.

It starts getting difficult in crowded harbours, when you've other boats and a strong tide to contend with. Which is why it's often best to pick up a buoy under power. Nevertheless, one day your engine may fail, so it's worth practising the manoeuvre under sail, in different conditions. If nothing else, it increases your knowledge of the boat, and gives you more confidence.

But first, as always, take note of what is happening. Which is stronger, the wind or the tide? It is no use meeting the buoy head to wind, if you are carried along, or swept past with the current.

So decide where the wind is coming from. Remember, your masthead fly only shows the apparent wind. Flags on shore or on stationary boats give a truer indication. And look at the way moored boats are behaving. You need all the clues you can get!

B. But, to start with, let us assume tide and wind are together, and you need main and jib to keep her under control. You approach on a run, then gently luff, up, to meet the buoy with the sails flapping in the eye of the wind. The hard part is deciding where and when you should actually start to turn. So much depends on the boat and local conditions. But practice in less congested water will have given you a better idea. As a rough and ready rule, you should start to luff with the buoy about two boat length's away, and level with your transom. The most common mistake is sailing too far down wind, so the boat stops too short. But it is as well to remember that that the turn should be gentle, rather than sudden or abrupt. If you spin round on the spot, everything happens so quickly, that the crew loses sight of the buoy, while the boat herself may even pay off on the opposite tack.

Some people like to drop the head sail when about three-quarters of the way through the turn, but that can sometimes cause more problems than it cures, particularly if the foretriangle is large and the boat small. With only two people on board, it occupies both of them, just at the most delicate stage of the operation. There's a good chance that, in trying to smother the sail with one hand, and pick up the buoy with the other, the poor, overworked foredeck hand will do neither very well. Of course, on a large boat, with plenty of crew, and space for them to move, it's a different story altogether. Either way, the skipper should make sure that the sheets are eased right off as the buoy is 'plucked' — and that the headsail is lowered smartly, to stop the boat sailing off again — once the warp has been secured. From all this, it is easy to see why, wherever possible, it is far more straightforward to pick up a buoy under mainsail alone.

C. The exception, is when the wind is against the tide. Here, the mainsail is a hazard, because, the wind will be behind you and it is impossible to lose power by feathering, at least with conventional rigs. You must approach under headsail alone then, and be prepared either to lower, or let it fly forward like a flag at the last moment, to make sure the boat loses way.

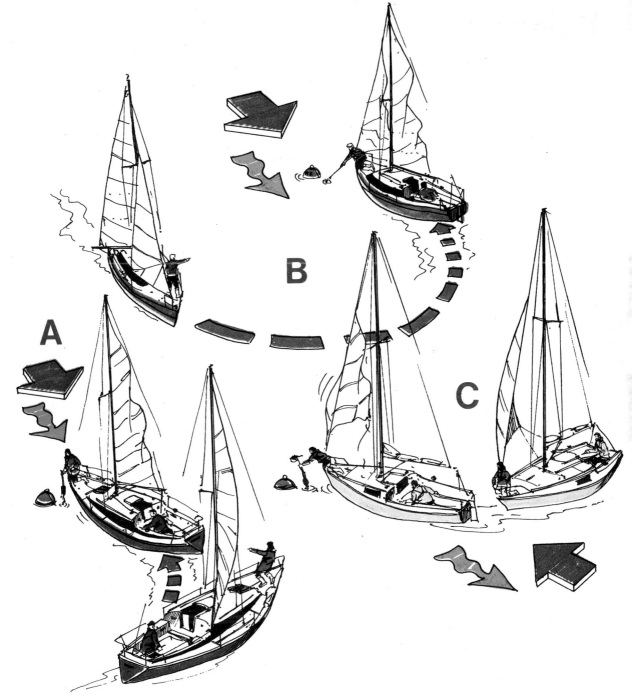

A

B

C

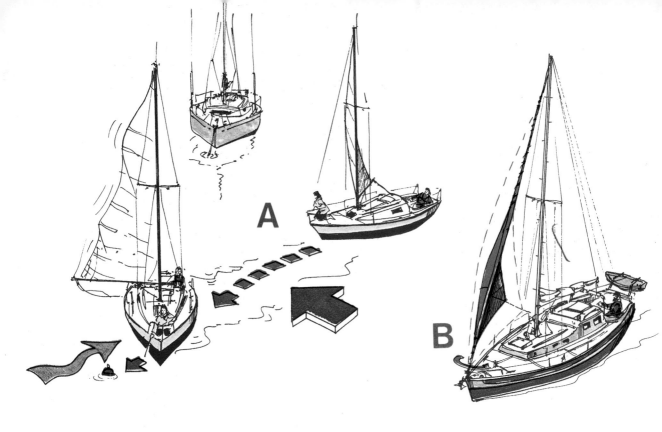

Wind across tide

Sometimes though, nature adds a subtle variation to provide us with wind which blows neither with nor against the current, but across it. Depending on its strength, moored boats will take positions at an angle somewhere between the two lines of force. That should be your final line of approach.

A. Come in under mainsail alone, with the wind aft of amidships, then gently round up, easing the sheet as you do so. The combined effect of wind and tide should hold you on course as you carry your way up to the buoy — but lower the mainsail as soon as possible to prevent her sailing off again.

B. When approaching down wind with a roller-reefing jib, you can adjust your speed by gradually reducing the amount of sail like a throttle. This device, of course, can also be used up wind, when it gets round the problem of actually lowering the sail — which, as we have already seen, can cause problems for the crew on the foredeck.

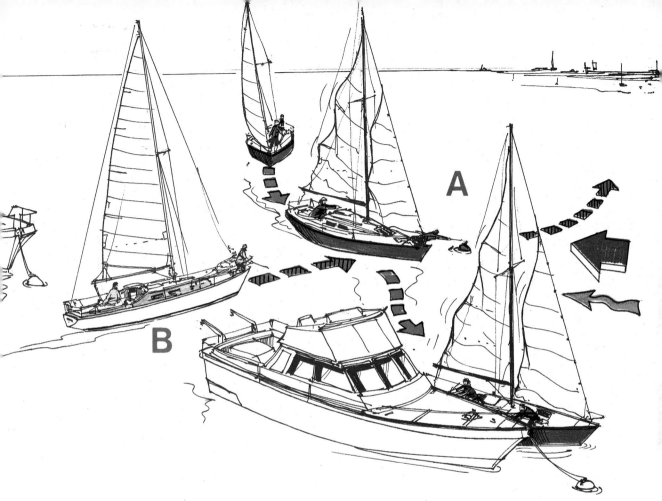

Everyone makes mistakes . . .

Successful boat handling is more a question of sizing up situations than applying hard and fast rules. Even so, mistakes happen, and no one is immune. All the 'experts' we asked admitted to some of the most dreadful blunders! So take heart and try to analyse what went wrong. Often it is a matter of rushing in without planning ahead. Always ask yourself: is the obvious way necessarily the best? Does it leave me any room if something goes wrong?

In the case of boat A, the answer is 'no' on both counts! Having misjudged their final approach, they miss the buoy, the bow blows off to leeward, and they end up entangled with a large, inconveniently moored motor boat.

But reaching in from another angle, like clever boat B, they could have sailed off into clear, open water, had their timing been wrong . . .

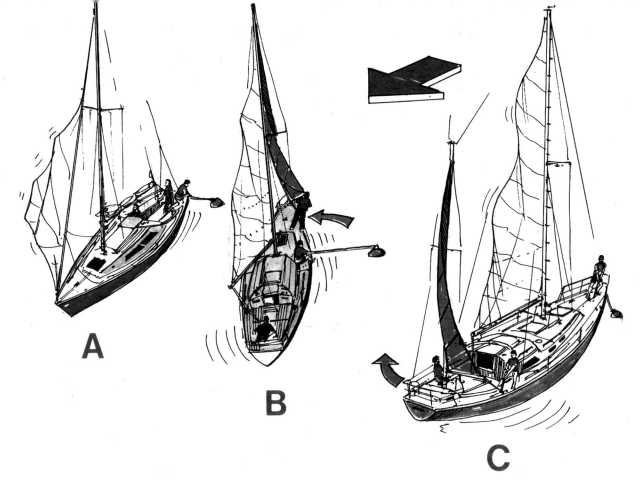

A

B

C

Leaving under sail

As with all manoeuvres, leaving a buoy under sail is something you should practice in open, uncongested water, though having said that, one should add that it is often easier than it looks, particularly if you want to move off with the wind behind you.

A. Simply rig an aft warp as a slip to the mooring buoy. Cast off from the bow, and heave in gently as the boat turns stern to wind. Hoist the headsail, sheet in, and release the slip at the same time.

B. To leave on the starboard tack, hoist main and jib, take a slip rope from the starboard bow to the buoy, and cast off the stemhead. By backing the jib, you can make the boat pivot, and turn to port. Slip the warp and sheet in.

C. On a two-masted rig, you can back the mizzen to turn her.

Do not always imagine you must sail off in the direction you are facing, particularly if the path ahead is congested. Apart from turning the boat, like (A), another option is to hoist sail, cast off, and drift backwards until you have enough room to make her pay off in the direction you want to go.

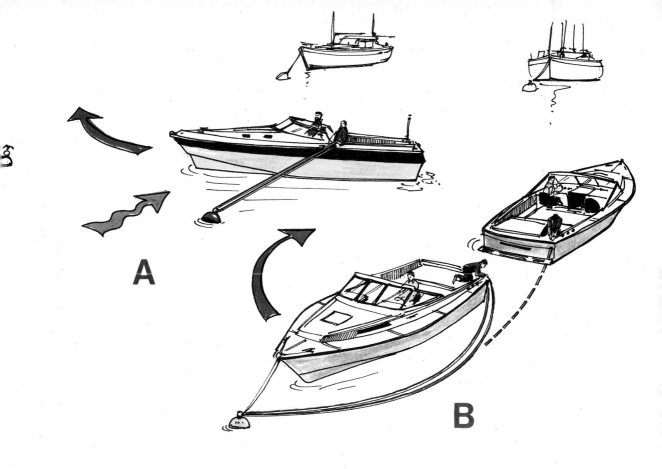

Leaving under power

How you react to this particular situation depends largely on the boat. Clearly, you are more likely to be concerned with warping techniques on a big, heavy sailing boat powered by a modest auxiliary, than you are on a twin-screw, turbo-charged race-boat! Even so, it is always a good idea to find out what wind and tide are doing, just in case something goes wrong. And even race-boats have their problems: for example, many are awkward to manoeuvre at slow speeds, and sudden bursts of power can be annoying to others, or in extreme cases, counter-productive. Whatever the situation, it is always more intelligent and prudent to have some regard to prevailing conditions, than to roar away, throwing caution to the wind.

A. As we saw earlier with the boat under sail, a slip rope round the buoy can be brought aft to alter your angle. The further aft you bring it, the greater will be the effect of the tide acting on the bow, and so, the greater the angle. Having 'lined up' the boat in the direction you want to go, motor ahead, and haul in the slip rope.

B. A slip rope taken from the transom to the buoy will turn the boat through 180 degrees when you cast off from the bow. It is a good idea to control the radius of the turn by hauling in on the slip, so her stern ends up where her bow was. The turn completed, you slip the line, and motor off in ahead.

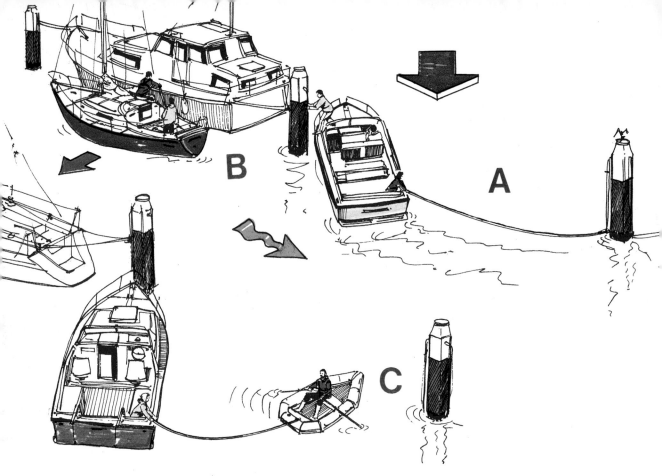

Piles: arriving under power

Pile moorings — large wooden stakes, usually with sliding mooring rings, driven into the harbour bottom, and arranged in rows. Unlike single buoy moorings, piles restrict both the movement of the boat once moored, and the number of alternative lines of approach when coming in to make fast. Having arrived, it makes sense to leave her with her bow pointing toward the ebb, if that is the stronger tidal flow. But listen to the weather forecast. With strong winds predicted, it might be safe to lie more in their direction. But first, the approach itself:

A. Motor up against the current with the stern warp brought up forward, and attach it to the down-stream post. Which side of the post you choose may be determined by the layout of the moorings, but if possible, approach to windward to avoid being 'pinned in'. Motor ahead, controlling the stern line to keep it clear of the prop, make fast the bow (see Chapter 11) then centre between the two piles.

B. If there is another moored boat already made fast to the piles, the manoeuvre is easier, since you have a larger target to aim at, and it is simply a question of coming alongside. Where possible, approach from leeward; apart from anything else, a leeward berth makes it easier to get off again. The wind will be helping, rather than holding you in.

C. If for any reason you feel unsure about getting a stern line to the down-stream post, moor to the upstream pile, then take the stern warp back in the dinghy.

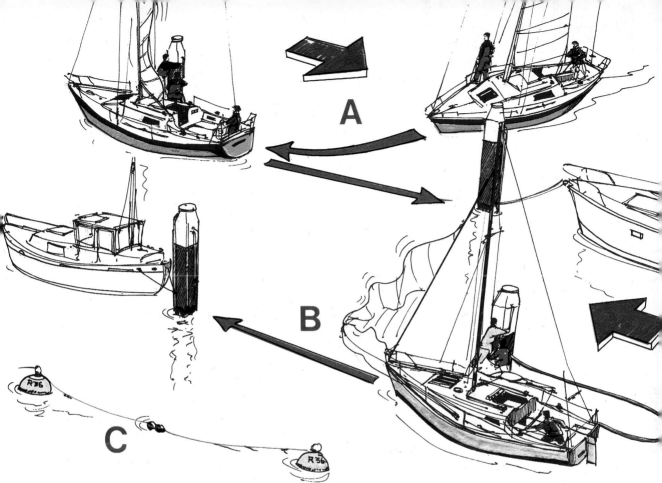

Piles: arriving under sail

A. Pile moorings are not designed with sail in mind. However, with the wind and tide together — and a well balanced boat — you may be able to sail in on a close reach under mainsail alone, and meet the up-stream post head to wind. You make fast, lower the main, and, in theory should then drop back on the tide, to meet the down-stream pile. In reality, you have a good chance of drifting back at an angle, in which case, you must take the stern warp to the post, in the dinghy.

B. Coming in against a strong tide, with a gentle breeze astern, is best done under headsail alone. On approaching the down-stream post, let fly the sheets, and make fast the stern line (brought well forward to make it easy). Sheet in the sail, and control your run to the up-stream pile by adjusting the stern warp.

C. Instead of piles, you may find fore and aft buoys linked by pick-up lines kept afloat with smaller buoys of their own. If so, approach it as you would a pier or pontoon (see Chapter 7). Fish up the line, and moor one floater-buoy forward, and one aft.

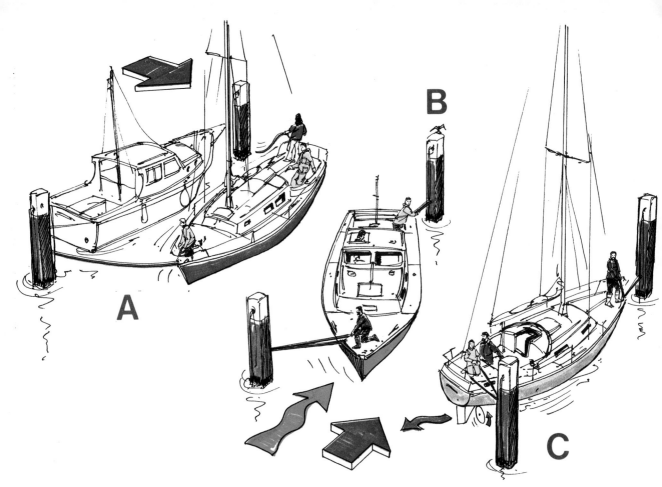

Leaving piles under power

A. When moored to leeward of another boat, the wind will help ease you off. Rig the lines as slips, then release the forward warp and let the bow drift out. When moored to windward, you may be able to make use of the current which will act on the hull and turn it, when the up-stream warps are released. But in strong winds or weak tides, it may be necessary to take a line out in the dinghy, and either make it secure to a point up-wind — or tie it to an anchor. You then haul yourself out. Alternatively, try rigging a spring as a slip, and motor against it. That should help slew her round (see Chapter 2).

B. When facing into wind and current, take the bow line down the inboard side to provide leverage, and sheer you into the stream.

C. Is she facing down wind and down current? If so, and she handles well in astern, ease the stern warp, and reverse, snubbing her on the bow line as you do so. Depending on which side you want to leave, prop effect may help you still further. If handling astern is suspect, warp her round and go out in ahead.

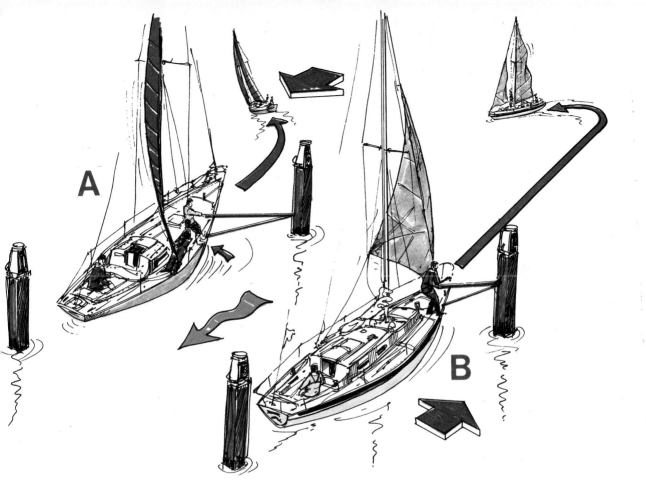

eaving piles under sail

This manoeuvre, like so many others, needs lots of practice. Funnily enough though, it is sometimes easier than leaving under power, since your sails may offer more leverage than a small, finely-cut prop. But in strong winds, of course that can be less of an advantage, particularly if they have the effect of 'pinning you in'. Even so, it is usually best to leave facing the current as that enables the rudder to work more efficiently.

A. Here, the main can be backed, or the bow line brought aft as a slip to help the wind and current ease

her out at the right angle. If you haul on it smartly, the boat will build up momentum over the current — which is just what you want. Once clear, you can hoist the headsail.

B. With the wind against tide, rig the lines as slips and hoist the headsail. Haul in on the bow warp to get her heading out across the current, then sheet in and sail away. Once clear, luff up, and hoist the main.

Make it easy for yourself (and others)

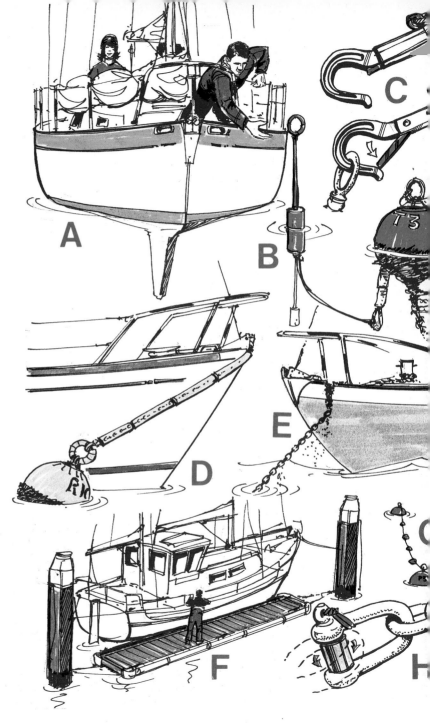

A. Women's lib or not, why not let your female crew (or mate) steer the boat while you tackle the more physical job of plucking the mooring itself?

B. A tall dan-buoy is easier to get hold of than something floating nearer the surface of the water.

C. A 'Grabbit' type boathook, which has a spring-loaded retaining bar, cannot slip off the buoy's eye once you have released the 'trigger'. But you can release the pole, leaving you attached by the hook, which is tied to your mooring line. It means you can pick-up the mooring single-handed from the cockpit.

D. Pad the buoy, its ring, and the strop, so it cannot damage your boat in rough weather.

E. Make sure the strop is well secured, by either a rope or pin, in a deep fairlead or bow roller — otherwise it may jump out and 'saw' through your topsides. It has happened!

F. A narrow pontoon secured between piles, keeps the boats apart better than fenders alone, and turns an awkward mooring into a relatively straightforward one.

G. The line between fore and aft buoys should be supported by small floats — to make it visible, and give you something to aim at . . .

H. Oversize metal tube on your shackle pins will revolve like rollers, and reduce wear and tear.

Coming alongside (7)

In common with most manoeuvres, coming alongside can be as simple or as difficult as conditions allow. For example: imagine yourself at the helm of a heavy displacement, single engined motor cruiser with right handed propeller. The wind is light, and the sea smooth. Away off the port bow is a floating pontoon, three times as long as your craft, and with no other boats attached to it. You throttle back. The 2½ knot tide running against you, reinforces the braking effect as you edge even closer, finally approaching, gently, at an angle of some 20 degrees, before giving a short burst astern, both to kick the after end round parallel with the pontoon, and kill all forward movement.

Alternatively, if the propeller were left handed, the pontoon shorter, with other boats moored alongside, and a strong wind blowing from the port quarter aft of amidships, the task would be harder. The paddle wheel effect in astern would only kick you away still further. In that case it might be advisable to creep in at an angle, then swing the bows out, so, with the after end closer to the jetty, a burst astern would paddle to starboard and turn the bow to port.

When leaving, plan it out first, and tell everyone what you want to do. Then there should be plenty of help to ease you out and close the gap behind you.

Then again, a fierce wind blowing straight off the pontoon or jetty, may encourage other variations on the conventional approach. The same applies to strong winds blowing you in; it might even be necessary to anchor off and ease your way back on the cable.

Under sail alone, with no mechanical braking effect to fall back on, your speed of approach is more critical. Too slow, as you luff or spill wind, and the boat may drop back; too fast, and the momentum may drive you on, perhaps with disastrous results.

Coming alongside

1. Do not leave your crew in the dark. Tell him exactly what you want to do, and how you plan to do it. Give him simple, straightforward instructions then continue to keep him informed. Make sure he does not block your view!

2. If you come alongside another boat, your first priority is to ask the owner's permission. He might be preparing for sea . . .

3. Use your eyes. Local conditions may be unpredictable, whatever the tide tables say. Close-in there may be back-eddies.

4. Are you drifting sideways? If you keep staring ahead, it is hard to tell, so glance astern from time to time, and check your relative position.

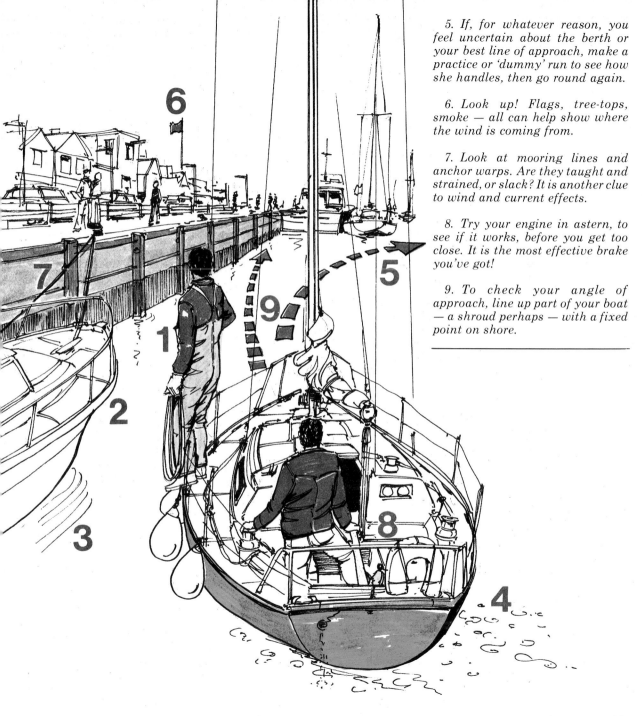

5. *If, for whatever reason, you feel uncertain about the berth or your best line of approach, make a practice or 'dummy' run to see how she handles, then go round again.*

6. *Look up! Flags, tree-tops, smoke — all can help show where the wind is coming from.*

7. *Look at mooring lines and anchor warps. Are they taught and strained, or slack? It is another clue to wind and current effects.*

8. *Try your engine in astern, to see if it works, before you get too close. It is the most effective brake you've got!*

9. *To check your angle of approach, line up part of your boat — a shroud perhaps — with a fixed point on shore.*

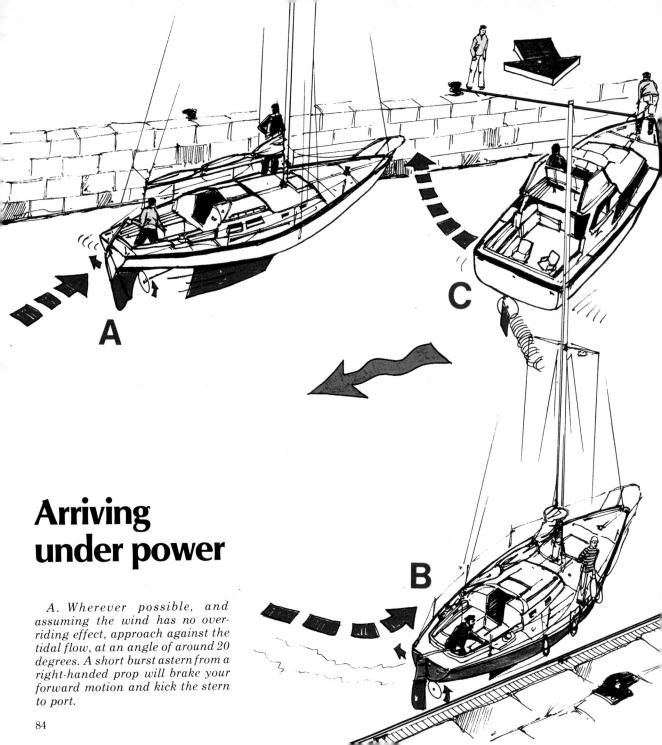

Arriving
under power

A. Wherever possible, and assuming the wind has no over-riding effect, approach against the tidal flow, at an angle of around 20 degrees. A short burst astern from a right-handed prop will brake your forward motion and kick the stern to port.

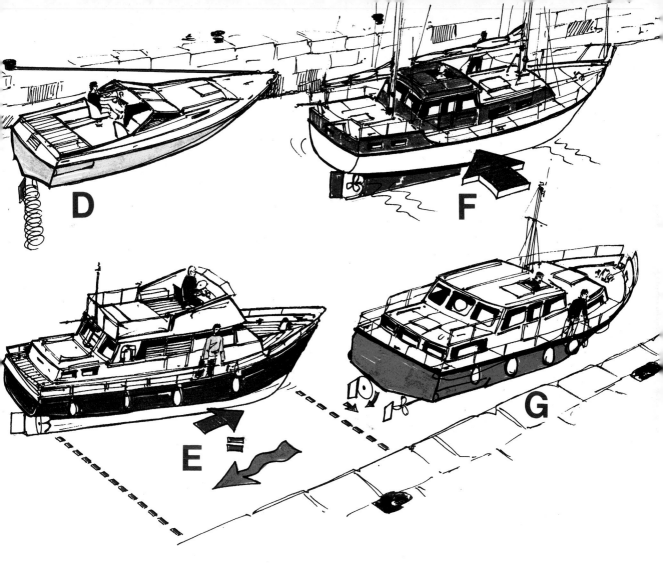

B. Here, a right-handed prop kicks you away from the berth, so turn out slightly, then straighten her with a short burst astern.

C. With a strong offshore wind, it might be safest to approach bows first, land a man ashore, and rig a spring from the bow, or ideally near the pivot point of the boat. This will ease you in when you motor gently ahead. But don't forget to protect the bows with a fender.

D. Once taut, the spring acts like a brake, and the boat, trying to take up the same angle, can be held close to the wall.

E. If the berth is small, it makes sense to 'walk' your boat sideways. Try adjusting the throttle to hold her steady against the current, ease the bows over, and the tide should push against the stern and edge you across (see Chapter 2).

F. An onshore wind can blow you sideways into your berth.

G. Most twin, handed, propellers revolve outwards in ahead, so by running the outboard engine in astern, the screw kicks the transom to starboard.

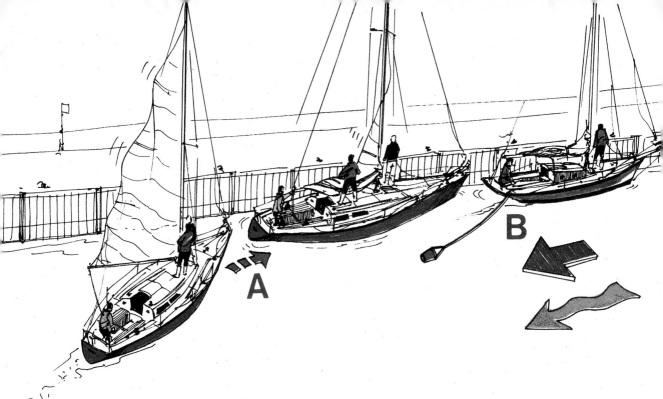

Arriving under sail

A. If your boat handles well under mainsail alone, coming alongside is often fairly straightforward, particularly when you have wind and current parallel to the quayside. Normally, you can slacken your speed by easing the sheet, but if for some reason, you still come in too fast, steer away and go round again. Should you undershoot however, drift back until you are clear of the berth before making another attempt. Once alongside, it's a good idea to lower the main smartly, not only to reduce flogging, but also to avoid the risk of it filling to some odd flukey breeze.

B. Some skippers drop a bucket astern to slow them down. But it needs to be strong . . . and, of course . . . practice makes perfect!

C. Coming in against the current, with a breeze behind you, it is impossible to spill wind from the main, so approach under headsail alone. Naturally, how much sail you set depends as much on the wind that's driving you, as the tide that's holding you back. It may pay to partially lower the sail, or to get the crew to hold it out — or, in really strong conditions, to lower away completely and approach under bare poles.

D. With an offshore breeze, you can either come alongside 'dinghy style' (D1), feathering the sail (or sails) to reduce way on the boat, or you can head straight in, and, keeping the boat moving, lower the headsail, luff, then lower the main, before surging up into the current, and getting a line ashore (D2). Which method you adopt depends on the boat. With a big, powerful yacht that carries her way, the second method is generally considered safer.

E. With a small boat and an onshore breeze, lower all sail, turn parallel to the quay, and let the wind do the work. A backed jib will provide extra 'push'.

F. But the larger the boat, the more the momentum, so it is sometimes safer to anchor off and ease her back gently on the warp.

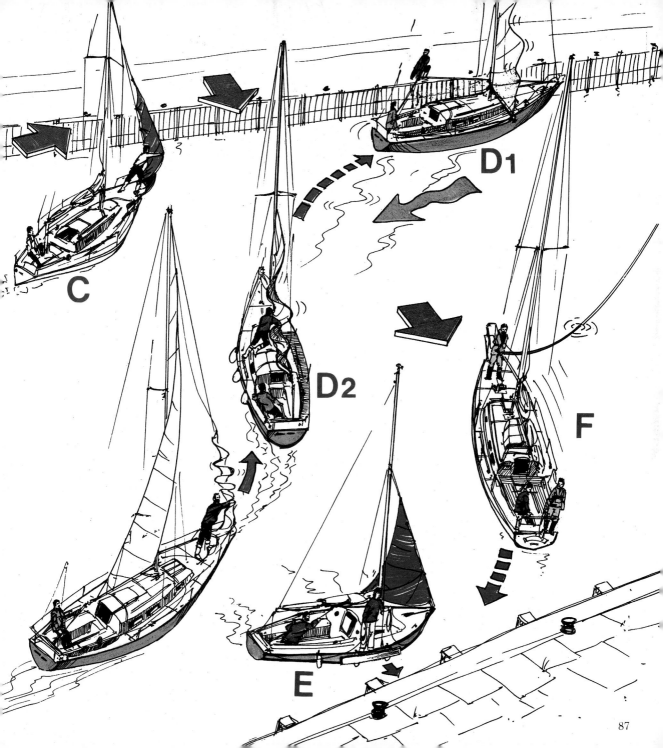

C

D1

D2

E

F

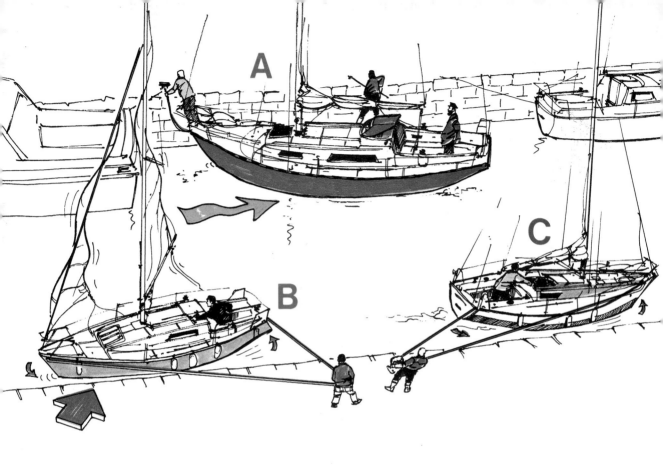

ALONGSIDE Stopping warps

A. Having motored alongside, against current and wind, all you need, initially, is a bow warp to stop the boat drifting back. The tide will push you in.

B. When coming in under full sail — which might be necesary if there is a strong tidal flow — get the crew to stand, with bow and stern warps, at a point where it is easiest to disembark (usually at the widest point of the boat). He should then hop ashore and take the bow line round a bollard (surging) — while, at the same time checking the stern line, to hold the bow off the quay. Lower the sails smartly, in case they back and fill.

C. Coming alongside with the current is potentially dangerous. For that reason, it should be attempted only if the you know how your boat will respond, and if your crew is quick on his feet. He must get ashore, and simultaneously 'surge' the stern warp, and tension the bow line, to keep her in close.

D. With a convenient (and strong) attachment point positioned about a third of the way forward, you can stop the boat with one line instead of two.

E. Slotting into a small gap is often best done by mooring up-tide, alongside another boat, then easing back on a warp.

F. A continuous line running from bow to stern, outside the shrouds, can be useful as a temporary brake if you are coming alongside singlehanded — particularly if your mooring has a handy bollard like this!

Mooring alongside

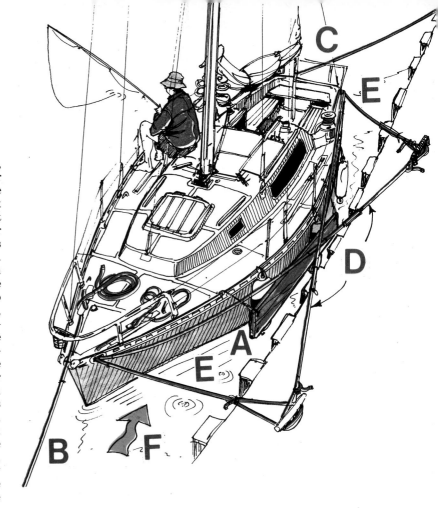

To save any last minute 'panics', it's a good idea to have all your warps sorted out and ready for use before you enter the harbour. Check with your crew that lines are fed out through fairleads, and back over the guard rails, to a point where it is easy to step ashore (see Chapter 11). And, since you may not know in advance which berth you'll be using, be prepared to moor either to port or to starboard. That means, among other things, having fenders on both sides, as well as a couple of spares handy which, if necessary, can be dropped in between the boat and the quay; it is much safer to stop a bump with a fender than your feet! And, since some quays are full of lumps and protrusions, another useful form of protection well worth considering, is the *fender board (A):* just a plank really, but it helps to smooth out any awkward irregularities. By the same token, why not keep the outboard fenders in place, just in case someone comes and moors alongside *you* . . .

Anyhow, having stopped the boat, the next step is to moor up properly, so you can either leave her in safety, or perhaps, even indulge in a spot of quiet fishing, like our friend on the right. As you can see, he's rigged *bow (B) and stern (C) lines* to hold her fore and aft, plus *diagonal warps (D) or 'springs'* so stop her sawing back and forth against the dock. The short lines from bow and stern are called 'breast' ropes (E) and hold her in towards the quay. Though some people leave them off, they do make it easier to climb to and from the boat. And it is as well to rig them if you are leaving the boat for any length of time, just in case another line gives way, *You might also attach the stern warp to the outer cleat, instead of the nearer one, which helps ease the bow round and, in so doing, allows the current to push the boat just clear of the quay rather than chafing tight up against it (F).* Of course, chafe in general is something to guard against, so examine your fairleads and cleats for any signs of sharp edges, and protect the warps where they cross the edge of the quay.

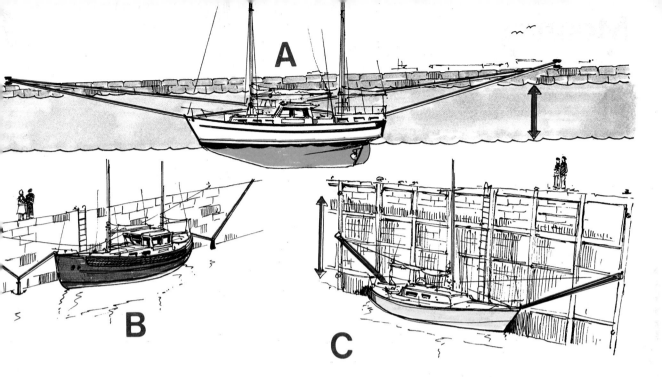

Tidal rise and fall

A. How to keep your boat reasonably tight-in against the quay, yet free to move up and down on the tide, is a problem which can only be solved by first knowing how far she will rise and fall. The next step is to multiply that figure by a minimum of three, to find out how long each warp should be. They should then be led well fore and aft of the boat so they can remain taut, and move through a narrow angle, as they follow the boat down. (Think of them as solid bars, hinged at both ends.)

As to the choice of material, nylon ropes are probably better than Terylene or Dacron in this kind of situation, because they stretch more. But try and protect them from chafe.

It also makes sense to have someone stay on board, to adjust fenders and warps, particlarly if you are in a strange harbour. The quay may be full of lumps and bumps; the tide may fall more quickly or more dramatically than you thought — a rope could even get caught on the way down.

B. You can also keep the lines tight by attaching a weight, say between 10 and 15lb. (4.5 to 6.7kg) mid-way down the line. An anchor or ballast pig would do.

C. Instead of attaching your warps to the top of the quay, you may fasten them to rings or cleats at the half-tide level. If you do that at low water, the warps will get slacker as the boat rises, but tighten up again on the top of the tide. At that point, of course, the rings will be underwater, so it is best to rig the lines as slips.

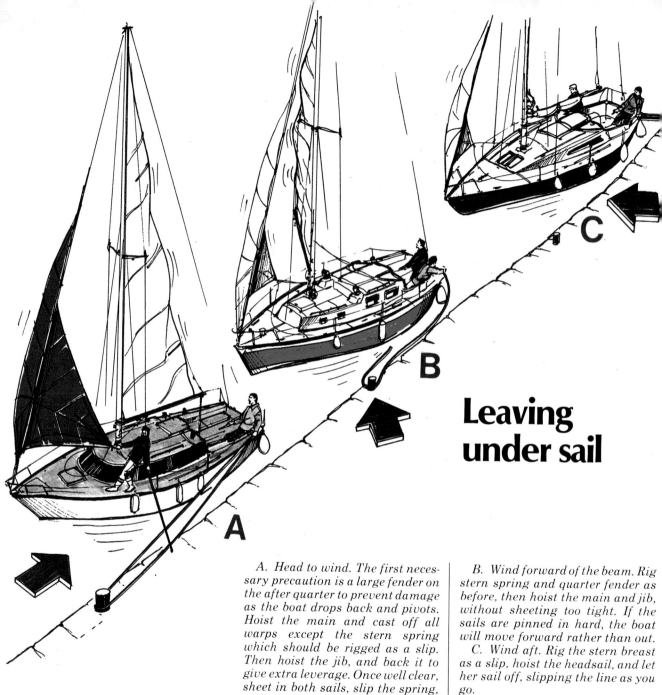

Leaving under sail

A. Head to wind. The first necessary precaution is a large fender on the after quarter to prevent damage as the boat drops back and pivots. Hoist the main and cast off all warps except the stern spring which should be rigged as a slip. Then hoist the jib, and back it to give extra leverage. Once well clear, sheet in both sails, slip the spring, and ease away.

B. Wind forward of the beam. Rig stern spring and quarter fender as before, then hoist the main and jib, without sheeting too tight. If the sails are pinned in hard, the boat will move forward rather than out.

C. Wind aft. Rig the stern breast as a slip, hoist the headsail, and let her sail off, slipping the line as you go.

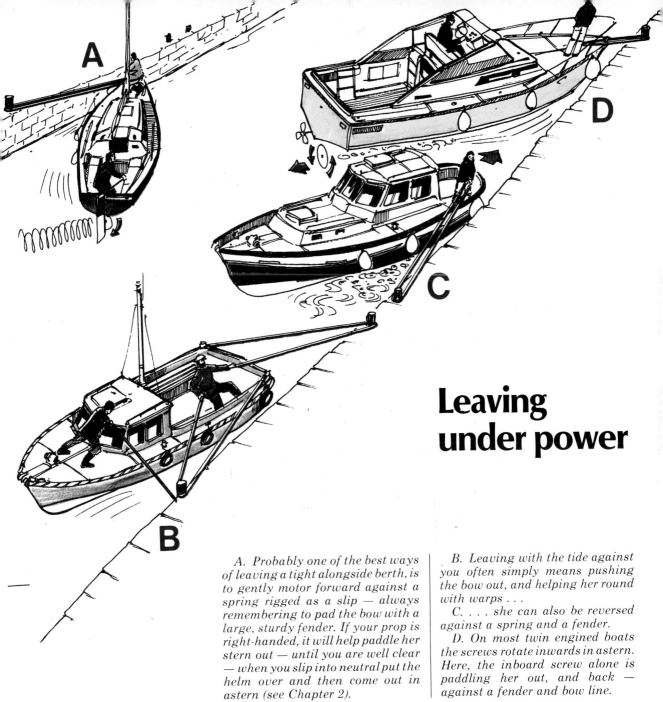

Leaving under power

A. Probably one of the best ways of leaving a tight alongside berth, is to gently motor forward against a spring rigged as a slip — always remembering to pad the bow with a large, sturdy fender. If your prop is right-handed, it will help paddle her stern out — until you are well clear — when you slip into neutral put the helm over and then come out in astern (see Chapter 2).

B. Leaving with the tide against you often simply means pushing the bow out, and helping her round with warps . . .

C. . . . she can also be reversed against a spring and a fender.

D. On most twin engined boats the screws rotate inwards in astern. Here, the inboard screw alone is paddling her out, and back — against a fender and bow line.

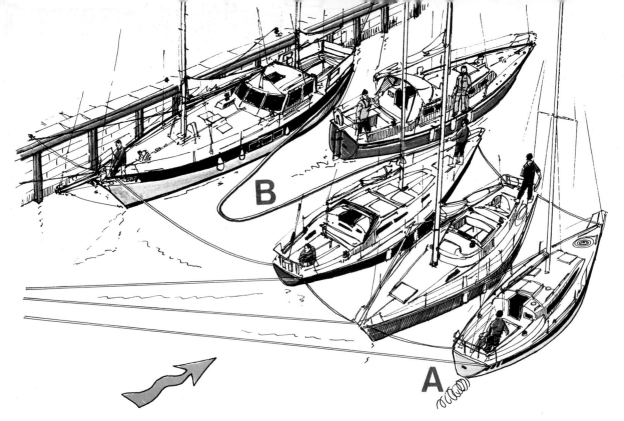

Rafting-up alongside

With harbours increasingly crowded these days, it may be necessary to moor alongside other boats — which, in fact, is often easier than squeezing into a gap. Apart from anything else, there will invariably be plenty of willing hands to help. Nevertheless, there could also be numerous 'comings and goings' taking place, so rather than committing yourself too early, keep your eyes open for signs of movement, and cruise gently up

and down to find the most suitable spot. It is usually safer to pick a boat slightly larger than your own, but in any event, ask permission first, have your warps and fenders prepared in the normal way, and look aloft to make sure your spreaders don't tangle with the rigging 'next door'. Once safely alongside, moor up with springs and breasts as before, ensuring that bow and stern lines are attached to the quay, otherwise there's an unfair strain on the next boat in line.

If you wish to leave from an inside position, good-will and team work will make the job easier; so will co-operation from other craft in the 'raft'. If you have a choice, it is probably best to edge out with the tide or wind (whichever is the

stronger) to ensure that the raft drifts back together again once you've gone. Still, as we've said so many times before, real-life is often more complicated and less obliging than 'text book' situations, so it is a wise precaution to have the outside boat start her engine (A); if the raft does begin to break up, she can nudge them back — like a sheepdog!

Before the inside boat leaves, she should cast all her lines free, and rig her breast warps as slips. The other boats' shore lines must, of course, be removed from her path, and a new line (B) rigged behind her, outside rigging and shrouds, then tensioned once she's clear of the gap, to drag the remaining boats back together. Their shore lines can then be re-rigged.

omfort

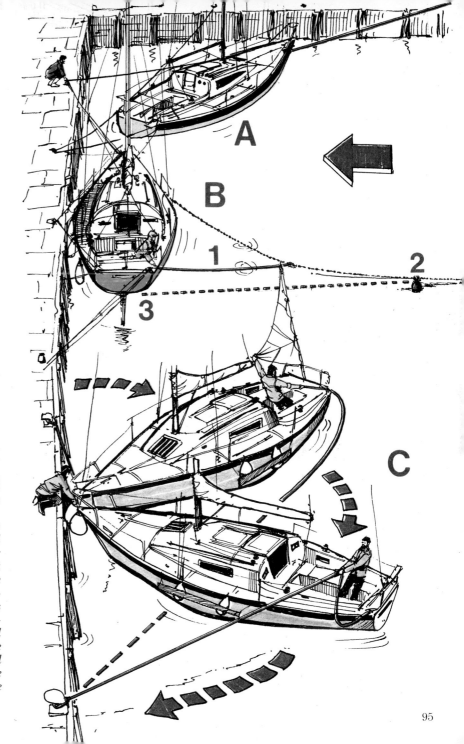

n exposed harbours with strong onshore winds, a berth alongside may not only prove uncomfortable; t can also damage your topsides. That being so, you may wish to move or readjust your position.

A. One alternative, if there is enough room, is to moor across the corner of a berth, with the lines tensioned so the boat stays away from the sides.

B. Another option is to hold her off with an anchor. Rather than securing the cables amidships, it is easier to form a bridle (1) by attaching a stern line to it. Naturally, in some harbours, this could be seen as a hazard to others, in which case, it might be advisable to run a weight down the cable (2) or rig it underneath your keel (3), to keep it low in the water.

C. Often though, wind is more of a nuisance than a hazard, and you may wish to turn your boat simply to make life a bit more comfortable. You should rig normal sized fenders on the opposite side, plus an extra large one at the bow which otherwise can crunch against the dock. A long stern line rigged outside, and back to the poontoon, will also be needed.

Cast off all warps except the forward breast rope, which will hold her bow in, and then push her stern out. Keeping her bow tight against the fender, let the wind take her round. If there's a current stopping her a small amount of canvas aft — on the backstay perhaps — will help. Otherwise, you could motor against a spring. Once she has swung past ninety degrees, pull on the stern line to complete the manoeuvre, and make fast (see Chapter 2).

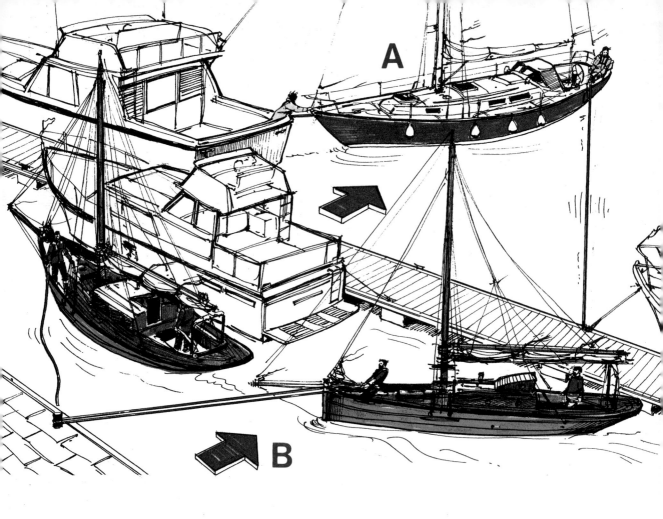

Coming alongside in strong winds

A. Slotting into a gap may be very awkward when there is a strong offshore wind to contend with, so, if you're not too sure about it, come slowly up to the next boat along and get a bow line on. Once secure, take a stern line ashore and, using the bow line as a pivot point, winch yourself in.

A strong onshore wind is even more tricky — and it's not a bad idea to get a line to a leeward berth or boat, if at all possible, then drop back on warps and under control.

B. Leaving a tight windward berth with a weak crew and engine can be impossible unless you take it easy and rig a slip rope to windward. Once you have walked or rowed the warp into position, haul the bow out, engage ahead and motor safely away.

Drying out alongside (8)

Making fast to a wall, quay or pier which dries at low water, is often more involved than would first appear. To start with, some boats, particularly those with tiny, angular fin-keels, are simply not suited to drying out, unless the bottom is extremely soft; even some twin keelers have a tendency to fall over if the ground is uneven; then again, your boat might have a skegless rudder or unguarded propeller shaft, both of which could be damaged as the craft settles down. In other words, it starts with knowledge of local conditions and characteristics of the boat in question.

Warps and springs must be sufficiently long to allow for the tidal range, and in extreme conditions may benefit from weights slid down them, to maintain tension and prevent the boat drifting out. To ensure the yacht settles down leaning in (by roughly ten degrees) rather than away from the berth, thus eliminating excessive strain on the lines, gear may be placed on deck, on the side nearest the quay. By the same token, a warp made fast on shore, in line with the mast, and secured to a block which can slide up and down a taut halyard as the boats drops, adds further control.

If you stay on board, keep aft of amidships. Too much weight forward may encourage the boat to settle down by the bow. She might even develop an awkward twist which will be impossible to correct. Naturally, single keeled boats are more prone to such disasters.

Does the bottom slope away from the berth? Are there hidden hazards — rocks or large holes? Prior inspection or consultation with local harbour masters will fill in the details. You should also study the quay itself. Are the sides smooth, or are there lumps and bumps to worry about? Will the fenders cope, or should you stay in attendance to obviate the risk of damage?

Once afloat again, you should make a systematic check of such things as engine cooling inlets and sea cocks, in fact, any component which could conceivably have become clogged with mud or grit.

Drying out alongside

1. Before drying out, have a word with the locals. Take advice from boat owners or fishermen who know the area well. Alternatively, anchor off, and study the scene at low tide and see for yourself.

2. Do not disrgard warning notices, even if they look old or out of date. If you are not sure what they mean, ask someone to explain.

3. Is the wall smooth-sided all the way down? That's another question you want answered before you move in and take the ground.

4. Is the bottom flat, or does it shelve away? Are there any underwater obstructions which might cause damage or upset the trim? As before, you should find out in advance.

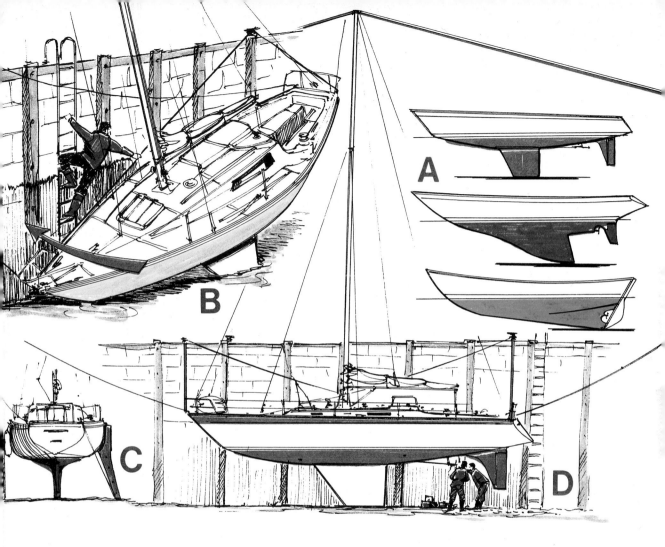

A. Some boats take the ground better than others. Motor boats, multihulls, centreboarders — and boats with twin or lifting keels — all should have little to worry about, other things being equal. But deep-keeled craft may be more of a handful. Short fin keels are particularly vulnerable since then concentrate high loads over a small area; if the bottom is soft and the weight unevenly distributed, they tend to dig in,

often at an angle. Sloping keels can also encourage an uneven attitude when the boat takes the ground. Or there may be problems with unprotected rudders or props. As always: first know your boat!

B. If she does tip forward, she may swing into the quay at the same time.

C. A drying-out leg will help keep her level, but only if the bottom is equally flat.

D. Boats with short fin keels can be encouraged to settle down level by setting up tight lines fore and aft. You can also extend the halyards from the masthead and make them fast on shore. In short, as long as they counteract and balance one another, the more ropes you use, the better and safer it is. But make sure they do not obstruct footpaths or roads . . .

Preparing to go down

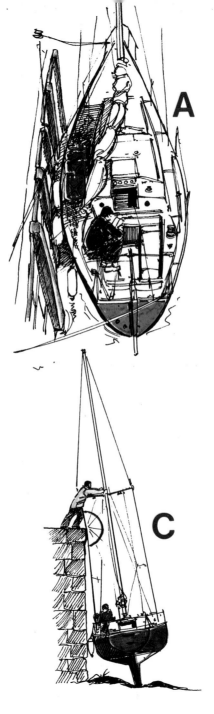

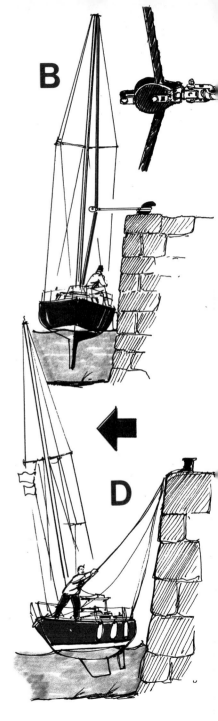

A. A slight lean towards the quay, which helps keep her steady, can be encouraged by placing heavy gear, like anchors and water containers, on the near-side deck.

B. A block threaded through a taut halyard, and attached to a line fixed to a bollard or cleat on the quay, will hold the boat in, as she slides down on the tide. It is a good idea to stay on board to check that all goes well, but remember, your weight could be critical, and she might take up a different attitude should you leave her to her own devices half-way through!

C. If you do stay on board, watch the shrouds for signs of chafe. You may have to disconnect them, so be ready with the tool kit! And make sure the fenders stay in place . . .

D. It may be calm enough on the boat, but a strong offshore wind could be raging just above your head, rattling the top of the rigging and heeling her over. Check it out. And do not forget to listen to the weather forecast. It might get worse!

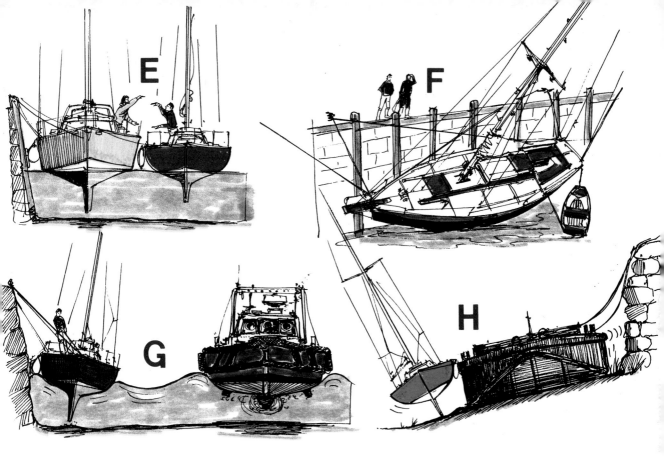

E. A boat moored on the outside, with less draft than you, will settle down and may drag you over. Ask the owner for details before you 'go down together'.

F. Have a good look round the boat and try to imagine what will happen when the water has gone. For instance: do not forget the dinghy, with too short a painter she might be suspended and acting as a weight to pull you over.

G. Is the water choppy; is there swell from passing ships? Remember, it may not take much to knock her away from the quay at the last moment — so wherever possible, keep watching and be prepared to take action.

H. However safe and stable they look, barges can be dangerous neighbours, particularly where a slippery, uneven bottom allows them to slide down on top of you. More than one yacht has been damaged that way.

Make it easy

A. Small strops mean you can secure additional warps to your cleats. But make sure your fittings are strong enough to take them.

B. Closed fairleads are best for drying out since they contain the rope at different angles, but it has to be threaded through. A fitting like this gives you choice.

C. Chafe-guards protect your boat.

D. Plastic tubing also reduces chafe in ropes, and holds them in place too.

E. Another way of restraining ropes is with lashings.

F. Cleats amidships mean your springs can be shorter.

G. A traditional samson post needs a cross-pin or bar to hold the rope captive when it is tensioned from above.

H. A strong fender-board spans buttresses and piles.

I. Fenders tied together in a clump can protect you from uneven quays.

J. A fender apron like this reduces the risk of scratched or damaged topsides.

K. A ratline or two (rungs in the rigging) makes boarding much easier . . .

L. . . . so do steps in your drying-out legs.

Marinas and Locks (9)

Marinas, with their regimented layouts, demand an equally disciplined approach from skippers whose use them. Clearly, the margin for error is less here than with swinging moorings, jetties or piles, where, in the event of a bad approach, you normally have room to swing away and go round again. A marina berth is often a cul de sac, with only one way in, or so it would seem. Small wonder that skippers sometimes feel forced into making mistakes.

Having said that, one should add that non-tidal marinas or those adequately sheltered from wind and current, are relatively easy to cope with; the real problems occur in more open, less protected sites.

For example: your berth may be down-wind and down-tide. Should you approach it with the engine in astern; should you anchor off, or should you come alongside a windward pontoon, either drop back on warps, or wait until slack water before making another attempt?

With a high-sided boat like this, it's a great help to have someone ashore who can take a line. You should also rig fenders which are both large enough to compensate for any flare of curve in the topsides, and sufficiently tough to withstand high crushing loads.

The third alternative is undeniably the safest, and for that reason alone must be preferred. It also points up the need to look out for options; to work *with* natural forces rather than *against* them, and to never feel compelled to undertake any manoeuvre that leaves too much to chance. The decision is yours, and sometimes, the 'correct' one is the hardest to make.

"No one likes admitting that a task is beyond them, but prudent skippers never accept unnecessary risks."

"No one likes admitting that a task is beyond them, but prudent skippers never accept unnecessary risks."

In awkward situations, you should ask yourself: is there another, easier berth and, if not, why not wait till conditions improve?

By the same token, while the ability to handle a boat, in restricted areas, under sail, is highly desirable, marina manoeuvres are best carried out under power. Indeed, in some marinas, that is the rule.

As for getting underway again, wind and tide may dictate judicious use of warping techniques. You might even set a small amount of canvas to help edge the boat off, or to turn her.

In some marinas, you anchor off and moor stern-to; in others you berth with the stern made fast to piles. Such variations are described fully, in the following chapter, along with their associated problems.

At the Entrance

1. *Finding the marina entrance can sometimes be embarrassingly difficult, so, as well as studying charts and pilot books in advance, have them to hand in the cockpit, preferably with a crew member acting as navigator, and using them for on the spot reference, as you concentrate on steering the boat.*

2. *You might also station someone high up, on the doghouse or coachroof, to act as a look-out.*

3. *Warps should be attached and 'ready for action'; fenders can be rigged on both sides if you have enough. It's also a good idea to have spare fenders ready to drop in between boat and pontoon, just in case things go wrong. For the same reason, keep the sails bent and secured with light lashings, and have the anchor prepared for use.*

4. *Don't forget to fly the right flags, particularly in foreign ports. Apart from anything else, it helps to create a good impression.*

5. *Look for signs of wind and current. Are flags drooped or fluttering; are mooring buoys upright or straining in the tide? Are there back-eddies or wind shadows?*

6. *If the situation looks really awkward or unclear, it might pay to ask, so long as you can get within hailing distance safely. But keep your questions simple and watch out for hazards like outfalls or fishing lines.*

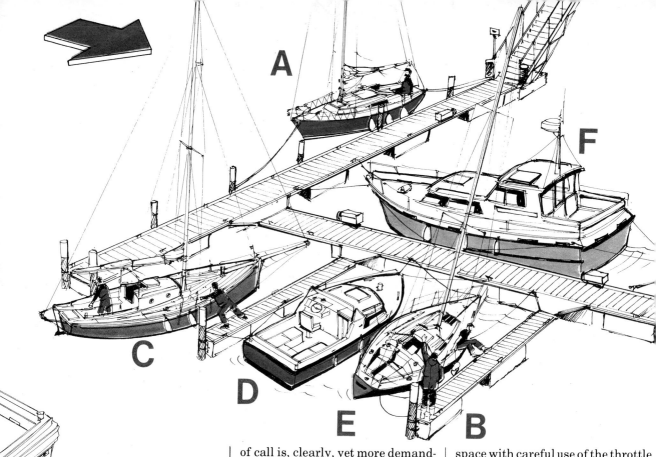

In the Marina

As already outlined, planning ahead is essential. Sorting out gear, equipment and crew, well in advance, leaves you free to concentrate on the next important stage: negotiating the marina itself.

Even if you know the harbour well, there may be problems with wind, tide or congestion, so never take things for granted. A new port of call is, clearly, yet more demanding, so try to find out as much about the layout as possible before you arrive. You should at least identify restricted zones or dangerous areas, whether there's a special place for visitors, or a one-way traffic flow system.

Having said that, you should still be prepared for the unscheduled and unforeseen; real-life is full of surprises! The visitors berths may be full; other skippers, trying to help you, may signal or wave, distracing you, maybe adding to the state of confusion.

Whatever happens, don't rush or lose control. If necessary, and if possible, keep your boat in plenty of space with careful use of the throttle in ahead and astern, before deciding where to go, and the best way to get there.

If there's no obvious gap, pick the most practical and easiest option. Be prepared for a temporary stop, alongside another, larger craft, for example, before receiving further instructions.

A. Some marinas have an easily accessible visitors pontoon or temporary landing stage, right near the entrance. You may be allowed to stay here overnight, or told to move on to some other vacant berth deeper in the harbour. Either way, it gives you time to think.

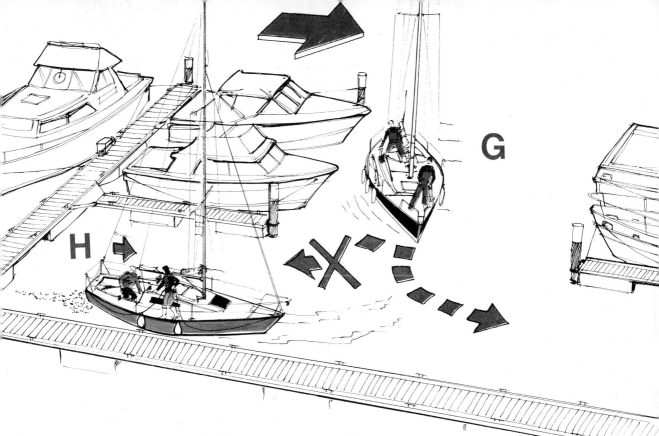

B. Alternatively, you may find an empty space, again, with a straightforward line of approach. Naturally, you should quickly report your arrival, since the owner may be on his way back. With sufficient crew, you can send someone to find out where to go, and then guide you in. He can also take your warps when you get there.

C. Watch out for other boats on the move, manoeuvring, or even getting into difficulties. Try to anticipate their problems as well as your own, and give them time and space.

D. If you do have a choice, remember that a leeward berth means the wind blows you away from the pontoon, reducing the risk of damage to your topsides.

E. A windward berth, in contrast, tends to keep you in contact.

F. When choosing between a berth which brings you head to wind, or one with the wind astern, the head-to option is usually the most comfortable unless you particularly want a cooling breeze in the cockpit.

G. Even faced with the luxury of choice, there may be limiting factors, like a strong wind, or the fact that your boat turns tighter in one direction than another (see chapter 1). Such inhibitions may even act in concert, the wind, for example, exaggerating the paddle-wheel effect of the propeller, making what, on the face of it, looks like an easy manoeuvre almost impossible.

H. With space so often limited, braking effects are particularly important in marinas, and it pays to know what your boat will and won't do. If, for whatever reason, performance in astern is weak — you might have a folding prop for example, it may be better to approach in astern, restricting her movement with short bursts in ahead; the greater control perhaps allowing you to edge closer to the berth of your choice.

Getting into a Berth

Having picked a berth, it's clearly a question of bringing the boat to rest in the desired spot with the minimum of effort. In ideal conditions, with no wind or tide, plenty of room, and an able and well briefed crew — and assuming you tackle the job gently — it's relatively simple. But in high winds, for example, or when manoeuvring short-handed, the obvious approach may not work, and different techniques will be called for. Naturally, it all depends on the situation; there's no way you can lay down hard and fast rules for every eventuality. Still, by studying the options and possibilities, you prepare yourself that much better, though, as emphasised and re-emphasised in previous chapters: practice is the key to success.

To simplify matters, our 'text book world' shows the wind blowing from left to right. With the tide in the same direction, you have but one line of force to consider, though real-life may be far less convenient. You should decide whether tide or wind has the greater effect on your kind of boat, then use it to the best advantage.

A. Never feel pressurized into difficult berths. If it's a tight fit, or means an awkward turn, for example, it might be better to moor temporarily at the end of the pontoon finger, before warping her round gently into position.

B. In the same way, you could come alongside another boat which, as a case in point, would be much easier than trying to squeeze up against the wind, into the vacant leeward berth shown here. Having made fast, you would ease her over with warps attached to the opposite pontoon.

C. Another windward pontoon, this time approached from leeward. By making a gentle turn and leaving enough space, you can let the wind do the work and simply drift into position. How much room you leave depends just as much on the strength of the wind as the drift

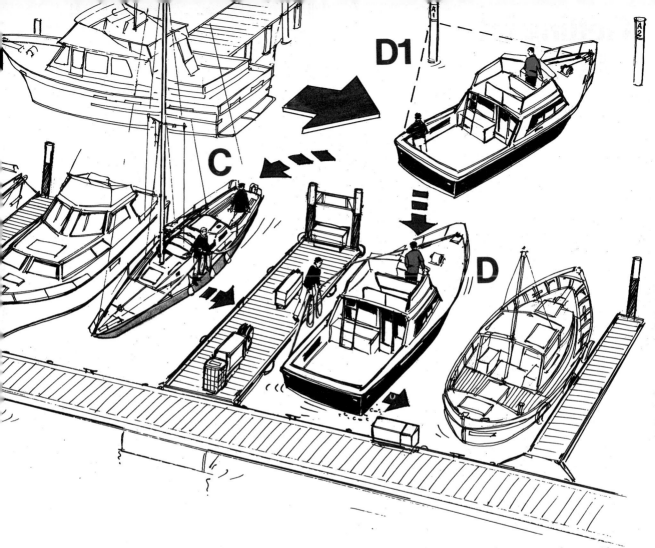

characteristics of the boat in question (see chapter 1).

D. Some boats, particularly motor cruisers, handle well in astern and can be 'backed in' like a car. Nevertheless, it always pays to harness what wind or tide there is, and use the prop effect to help as well. You can also give the odd controlled burst ahead, to slow down or change the angle of attack.

D1. But perhaps she has too much windage or not enough power. In that case, you might drop back on warps. It all takes time, of course; for one thing you must get the warps back afterwards! But that's better than damaged topsides.

E. Berthing with the wind aft and the engine in astern to slow you down, is potentially the most dangerous line of approach, and should only be attempted after prac-tice in safer surroundings. Above all, you need to know about prop effect and how much reverse thrust engine and prop can produce. All the same, with experience and a nimble crew, it may be perfectly possible to ease in under control and get the warps ashore swiftly, even if in extreme conditions, it demands cool nerves and sense of timing. So, if in doubt, pick an easier spot.

Leaving the Marina

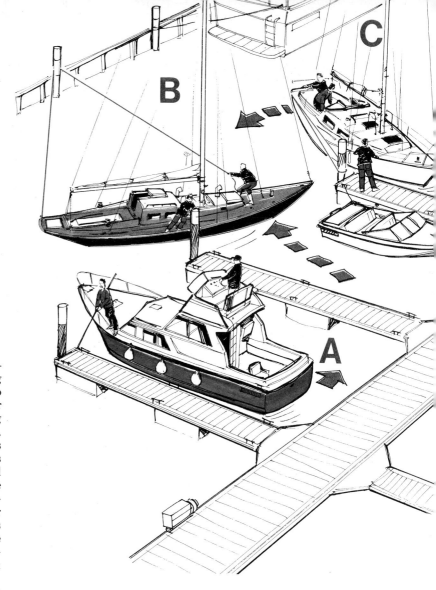

Leaving a marina berth is generally much easier than manoeuvring into one since you've more space to aim at! Quite often, it's just a matter of warming up the engine, slipping the warps and drifting away. Nevertheless, there will be times when conditions demand a less casual approach. A strong wind may pin you in tight; there could be other boats moored ahead, or insufficient room to turn under power alone. As before, given problems like these, it makes sense to figure things out slowly before committing yourself to precipitate action and unnecessary damage.

Quite often, particularly when the main problem is simply one of traffic congestion, it pays to wait patiently until everything's calmed down and sorted itself out. It's also important to brief everyone clearly, so they know exactly what to do, and can act positively without getting in each others way.

A. Moored head to wind, all you have to do is release stern warps and springs, then have the crew slip the bow line and push off the bow with a firm, positive shove, perhaps with the aid of a boathook. In ahead with a right-handed prop, the stern will move out to starboard, straightening the boat up and clear of the berth.

B. With a small or inefficient auxiliary, and no room to turn, it might be best to warp the boat off by taking a slip rope round a convenient post to windward, even if it means a long walk to set it all up!

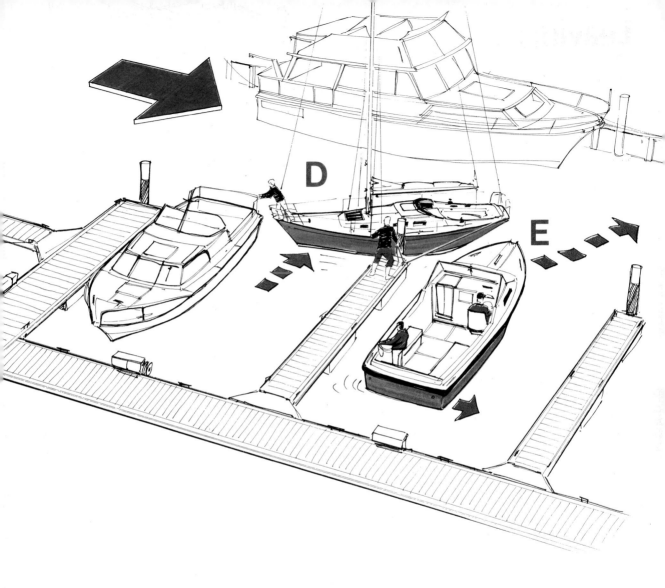

C. If she does handle well in astern, it might be possible to use wind or tide, plus prop effect, to power out backwards. In that case someone should watch the bow to prevent damage as the boat turns. A stern spring will prevent her going too far and tighten the turn.

D. Much the safest way of leaving a tight windward berth is to leave the engine in neutral and drop back on the warps, then use a stern spring to turn her while fending off the bow.

E. A beam wind and space to leeward is the easiest situation of all. Slip the warp, drift away in neutral, then motor off in ahead. A right-hand prop will also help to push the stern out.

Mooring stern-to

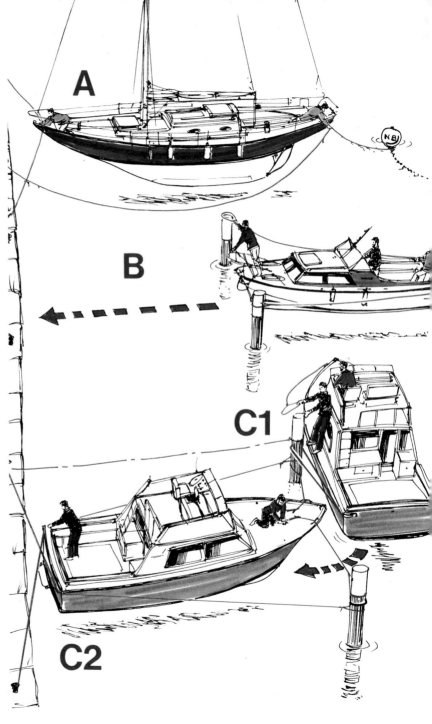

A. Some stern-to moorings are much easier to cope with than others, chiefly because they provide permanent attachments, like a moored buoy, to seaward, so you don't have to anchor off. Sometimes a sunken line joins the buoy to the wall, and should be fished up with a boathook as you slide in (bows first is simplest), before it can foul your prop. For the same reason, when leaving, make sure the line sinks properly before you start off.

B. Instead of a buoy, there could be piles. Slotting between them in astern should be fairly simple in light airs with a reasonable engine but otherwise approach bows first for safety.

Prepare warps and fenders in advance and bring two stern lines well forward. Attach them to the posts as you pass, and adjust them as you close on the wall.

However good your control, a dumpy bow fender is a wise precaution, just in case!

C. A wind parallel to the quay makes it easier to manoeuvre at ninety degrees to the post and secure a bow line.

C1. With a right-handed prop kicking to port in astern, you may then simply pivot into position. For a tighter turn, attach a stern line to the same post. Look out for lines between piles and quay. They are there to guide you in.

C2. Fix a large fender aft to protect her, cross the stern lines over, and run springs back to hold her safely in position.

Leaving

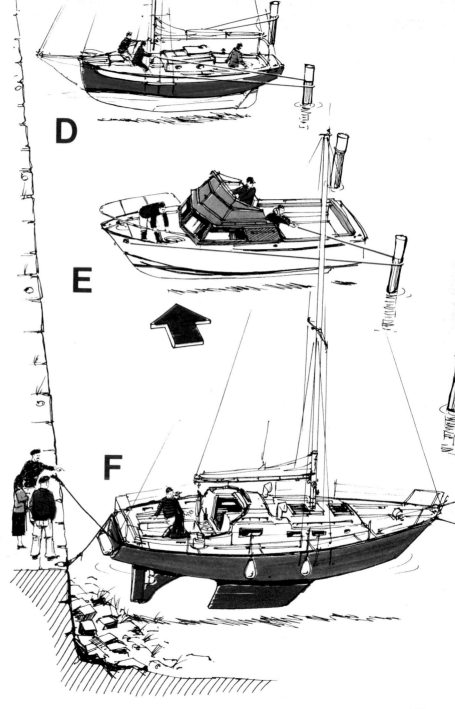

D. Boats moored close either side can be used to pull yourself back by hand. Otherwise, and assuming a wind parallel to the berth, you can rig long slips forward of amidships, and drag yourself out.

E. A beam wind calls for an aft spring, which you slip when you reach the pile, to stop her head blowing off.

F. Mooring stern-to makes boarding much easier but may mean loss of privacy. The risk of damage to rudder, self-steering and stern gear is also much greater should the weather turn nasty; all of which may influence your decision about which way round to make fast.

Anchoring stern-to a Wall

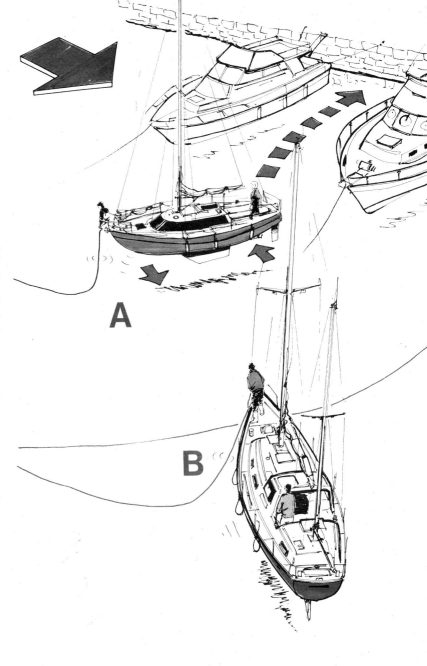

This manoeuvre looks difficult and, sad to say, quite often is! Combining anchoring technique (see chapter 4) with handling under power, usually in relatively restricted areas, it's at best a two-stage procedure, and calls for positive control. Given sufficient space, of course, the problems diminish. You can motor out from the wall, the reverse back gently in astern, dropping the anchor and letting the cable run free as you fall back under tension and slot into place. In reality, there simply may not be enough room, which means you must anchor with no way on the boat at all. Strong winds may complicate matters further, so could a weak or inefficient engine. For those kind of reasons you may find it safer, initially, to come in bows first using a stern anchor as a brake.

A. With little or no way on the boat, the rudder has minimal effect particularly in astern, so make allowance for wind, tide and prop effect. That may mean anchoring above or below the berth rather than directly ahead of it. If she still falls back off target, snubbing the anchor may straighten her. Or try a short burst ahead.

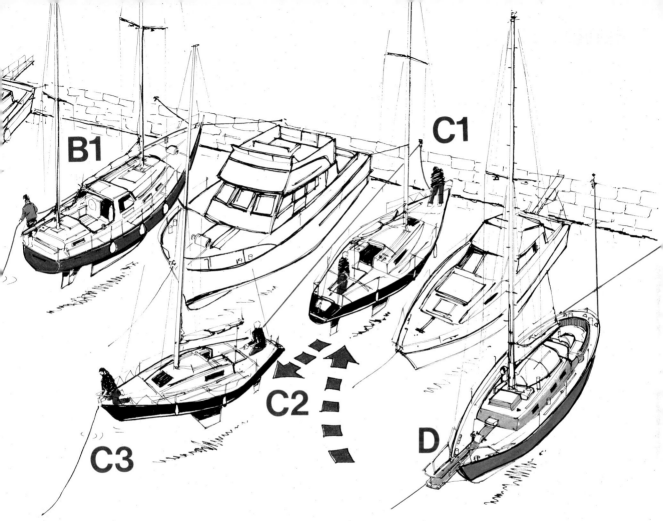

B. For numerous, self evident reasons, mooring bows on may be easier. And you don't necessarily have to anchor directly from the stern.

B1. By anchoring from the bow and taking the cable back round the outside to the stern where you then make it fast, you avoid having to lift heavy gear from one end of the ship to the other. Then simply motor in using the anchor as a brake.

C. But perhaps local regulations stipulate a stern-to berth?

C1. If so, you could motor in bows first and attach a long forward line to the wall.

C2. Reverse out and anchor.

C3. Then take the shore-line from the bow cleat and make it fast and the stern, and ease back under fore and aft control.

D. Having berthed safely, take stock of the situation and adjust your lines accordingly. In exposed positions, allow twice as much scope on the cable as normal; that makes it easier to haul yourself

clear of the wall in heavy weather or when it's time to leave. Crossing over the stern warps keeps her straight. But make them long enough to cope with local tidal ranges. It's also a good safety measure to rig up a tripping line on the anchor and check it every time someone leaves. A neighbouring yacht may inadvertently hook or dislodge it. And don't leave the boat unattended any longer than you must. A lot can happen in a short time!

115

Locks

Ideally, you will have already acquainted yourself with the particular system of signals in operation, and arranged warps and fenders on both sides of the boat.

Where you have a choice, it's best to keep well away from the gates where currents and eddies are likely to be strongest. Similarly, it makes sense to take up a position where the wind will hold you off, rather than against the wall — particularly important should the lock fill to the brim, when the turn of your bilge may be vulnerable.

Precisely how you make fast while you 'lock in' depends to a large extent on the facilities provided. There may be long vertical bars, chains or weighted ropes, running from top to bottom, or rows of pins, around which warps may be passed — though some locks are less well equipped, which means you must either heave a line up to the lock keeper, or take it with you up a slippery ladder.

In small locks it's usually just a matter of holding on by hand, but in larger ones, where you have commercial vessels churning up the water with their huge propellers, or where you have powerful sluices, you need to be more secure.

A2

A1

A. One of the easiest ways to moor alongside is to:

1. Bring the stern warp forward to the widest part of the boat, rig it as a slip, and take it back to the cockpit.

2. Motor forward with the bow line led back to a point on the boat where you can reach the wall, snubbing the stern warp to reduce momentum, if necessary. Adjust the tension to centre the boat between the two lines.

B. With no obvious attachment points, lines must be sent to the top of the lock, preferably with large eyes, to make them easier to secure. In practice, once through the gates, you slip into neutral and come alongside a ladder so the crew can climb to the top. Throw up the stern line with plenty of slack in it to compensate for any forward motion, then throw up the bow line and readjust the stern line to suit. With practice and preparation, the skipper can handle both lines unaided, but usually the man 'up top' tends the bow line. Closed fairleads simplify matters, and it can also help if you snub the lines round a winch. And remember, the bow line takes most of the strain when the sluice gates open.

C. It's not always so complicated though, and given a small, packed lock, you may find climbing or heaving lines unnecessary, and merely make fast to other boats with bow and stern warps. If so, try and pick one of the larger vessels to lie alongside, remove all vulnerable fittings — like pulpit-mounted navigation lights for example — and rig as many fenders as you possibly can!

Make it easy for yourself

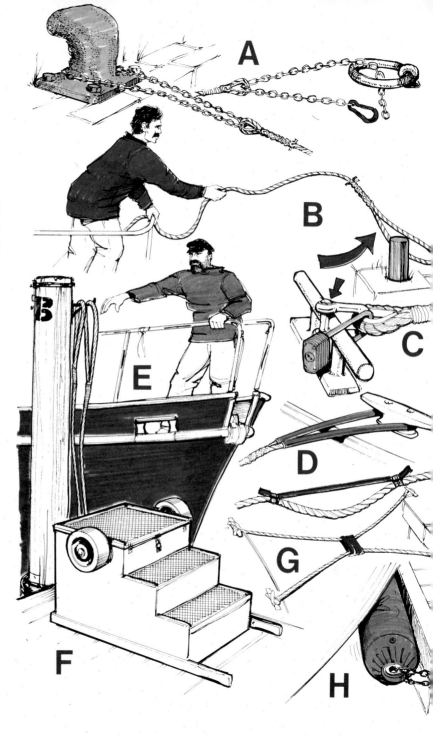

A. A chain loop on the end of a line adds weight which makes it easier to throw. It also resists chafe and, when fitted with a carbine hook, can be attached to rings as well as bollards.

B. It's not difficult to flip a loop off a bollard, so long as it's not too tight.

C. It saves time if you leave your dock lines already made up, ready for your return, but to make sure they stay there, rivet over the shackle pins. Some people even use padlocks . . .

D. Plastic pipe protects, and resists chafe.

E. Can you reach your dock lines? It may help if you hang them on hooks.

F. Getting a line ashore from a high sided boat is easier with steps or a dock-box. When you turn it upside-down, this one turns into a trolley.

G. A length of rubber fixed to your lines. Keeps then tight and absorbs shocks.

H. A large fender lashed to the dock will protect your stem. One day you might need it . . .

When things don't go right (10)

Anticipation is the best defence against mishaps. If you imagine the sort of things likely to go wrong when manoeuvring, you can build up a flexible set of responses.

For example: what happens if your engine fails? Naturally, it depends why, and in what situation. So you should ask the question often: approaching a buoy, stemming a tide, coming alongside. Imagine what you would do. Can you raise the jib from the cockpit? Where will she drift? Look around, and visualize.

Equally important is a knowledge of the engine itself. There may be time to rectify the problem if you have a good idea of what it might be.

Sails too, can be troublesome. A slide may stick when the mainsail is half way down; one reason why you should make the decision to drop sail and motor well in advance, in plenty of space.

It may be necessary to climb the mast to free a jammed yard or gaff; not something you want to do without having perfected it beforehand, in harbour. You should also carry basic tools like a shackle opener and knife, with you, at all times. When a rope must be cut quickly, there may be no time to fumble below in a locker.

Just as important is your attitude to those who sail with you. It helps to change roles regularly, rather

119

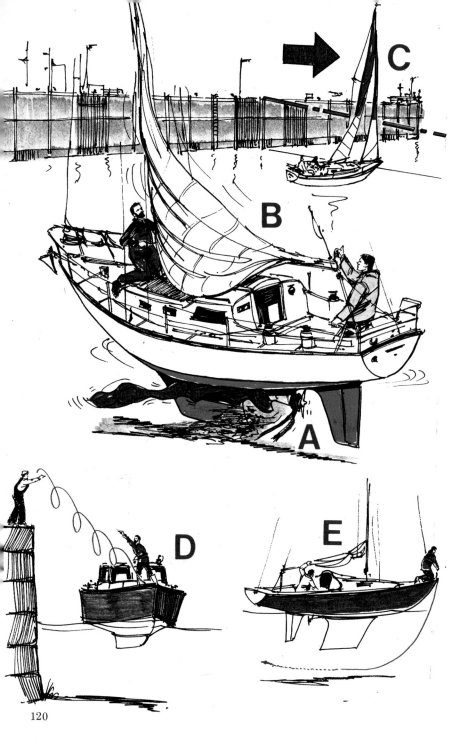

than alloting specific tasks to the same people. If someone gets injured — you might be taken sick yourself — the fact that the crew can cover for each other, may avert a disaster. With that in mind, you should always involve you crew, discuss potential problems with them, inviting observations and suggestions, they try putting different procedures into operation. Only by increasing individual responsibility will you encourage the kind of self-motivated sense of purpose which becomes absolutely vital when things begin to go wrong.

In this way, you may also reveal shortcomings in the boat and her fittings. One particular rehearsal may highlight a shortage of fenders, or the need for a larger cleat; you might need more chain, or some device to stop her bow blowing round with the wind.

As already emphasized, there is no substitute for imagination, common sense, and practice.

Even a well maintained and usually reliable engine can fail.

A. Mud, stirred up from the bottom and plastic bags can block water inlets; ropes, nets and plastic sheeting can wrap themselves round propellers — and bring you to a halt.

B. But whatever the cause of the problem, it pays to have the sails 'ready for action' rather than stowed down below in a locker.

C. In sheltered harbours it is often necessary to hoist either full sail, or at least ensure that you have enough area 'high up', to compensate for wind shadows.

D. It also pays to practice rope throwing, and . . .

E. . . . anchoring techinques. They can be used to great advantage when further controlled progress becomes either dangerous, undesirable, or impossible!

What do you do?

Your engine stops and there is no wind. What do you do? It is often tempting to anchor — but before you do anything, size up the situation. Note precisely where you are, what's happening to the boat, and what effect any course of action may have. If you do anchor, how much scope will you need, and where will the boat end up? Will you find yourself in the middle of moored boats (A) for example? If so, it might be better to let her drift out of danger and into clearer water. So take a couple of rough bearings to see in which direction you're moving. Are there are obvious hazards? Watch out for large, main channel buoys (B) indicating shipping lanes. And, of course, watch for ships themselves (C) and keep out of their way. Is the tide rising or falling? If you drift into shallow water (D) will you be left high and dry? And as always, study moored boats, smoke, even ripples on the water; it is all useful information which can help you make the best possible choice — or at least prevent an awkward situation from getting any worse!

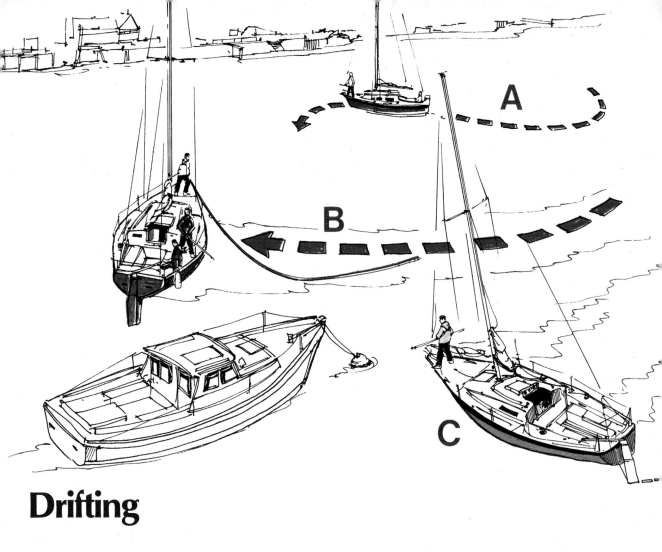

Drifting

If, for whatever reason, you have no obvious means of propulsion, and the boat begins to drift, your first immediate priority is simply to keep out of trouble. If there is any wind, it will have some effect on the rigging — enough perhaps to provide some small degree of steerage.

A. As you 'sheer' across, the force of water acting against the hull and the rudder, will invariably enable you to change direction slightly, which could be all that is required.

B. Alternatively, you can drop an anchor on a short scope or, better still, a length of chain from the bow (drudging) which, once on the bottom, acts as a makeshift brake, and may give just enough grip to slow down and change your 'angle of attack' when you alter the rudder.

C. But even without drudging you can slow down by keeping her beam-on to the wind — which offers maximum resistance. Here, as you can see, the tiller is lashed to leeward to help prevent her bow sagging down-wind. The crew stands guard on the foredeck, while the skipper mends, or tries to mend, the engine. Let us hope the problem is a small one!

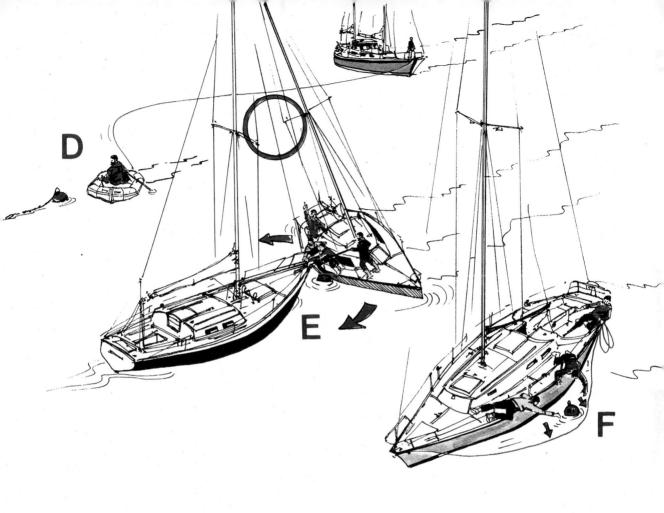

D. Clearly, you cannot drift forever, and if there is no obvious escape route, it makes sense to think about mooring — perhaps by getting a line to a buoy from the dinghy. As always do not forget to wear a buoyancy aid or life-jacket, then row or motor ahead of the boat to the most suitable 'target'. Having made fast, it's then a question of hauling in from the mother ship, while trying to limit or control any tendency to swing or pivot into danger.

E. If you drift down on another boat, remember, if everyone tries to fend off on the same side, the boat may heel and tangle her spreaders. So stay calm and tell people exactly what you want them to do. If the rigging gets hooked, you might be able to 'steer' or sheer the moored boat across the tide, which could be a help. So get a man aboard.

F. An old but effective trick is using a bight of rope to scoop up a buoy. Any non-buoyant warp will do, though some people attach weights so it sinks deeper, making it easier to catch the chain or line beneath. Once over, bring both ends of the line to the bow, so she lies to a long loop.

Sculling

Modern diesels are generally well engineered and reliable. Modern sailcloth is tough, light, and resilient. But when the gods conspire, even sophisticated, twentieth century hardware can fail — and, what is worse, may be difficult to fix. That is why many yachtsmen take more than a passing interest in more primitive and alternative methods of propulson. Since sculling relies on 'low tech' components which are cheap and easy to repair, it makes obvious sense. It also brings back a feeling of 'self determination' — well, as long as the weather holds out! In fact, when the wind drops, it is surprising how large a boat you can drive through the water this way. And to be realistic, that is the time you need it most. With an engine out of action, and no wind, sculling is a sensible solution.

There are several different methods, the most common of which is

A. similar to the dinghy technique already outlined in Chapter 5, but with a much longer oar (or sweep). It is best to mount the rowlock at an angle of about 45 degrees, since that helps hold the oar in the most efficient position. Keep your wrists underneath, and learn to use your body weight to counterbalance the rhythm of your arms, so you swing back and forth, harnessing timing and leverage rather than sheer muscle power, to build up momentum and drive.

B. Another slightly more developed version is one used by Bahamians, which means the skipper faces forward and can see where he's going. The sculling notch is offset, usually to port, so you scull with your left hand, keeping your right hand free for more important jobs. The main thrust is delivered on the 'pull' stroke, which counteracts the natural bias of having the oar to one side — while the shape of the long, narrow blade, with its 'diamond' cross-section, has an inbuilt tendency to flip over at the end of each stroke — all by itself!

C. More complicated to set up but, in return, even more 'automatic' is the oriental method, which uses a 'cranked' or bent oar for leverage, and a 'yuloh', or pin, instead of a rowlock. As you can see, the hole in the oar is tapered, so the shaft — and therefore the blade — can rock from side to side as it moves across the boat. It goes without saying that the precise degree of taper is crucial to the success of the whole operation. In practice, you push the lanyard with one hand, which twists the oar to the right angle, following with a push on the oar itself with the other. You then repeat in the opposite direction. But, as we said before, the big attraction of sculling is simplicity, so don't let's forget that dinghy oars can be lashed together or, better still, a 'stand by' blade . . .

D. . . . can be made beforehand to fit onto the spinnaker pole. And you can always row with your makeshift oar, by tying a loop round a winch to form a rowlock.

E. Keep her straight by steering with the tiller wedged snugly, like so . . .

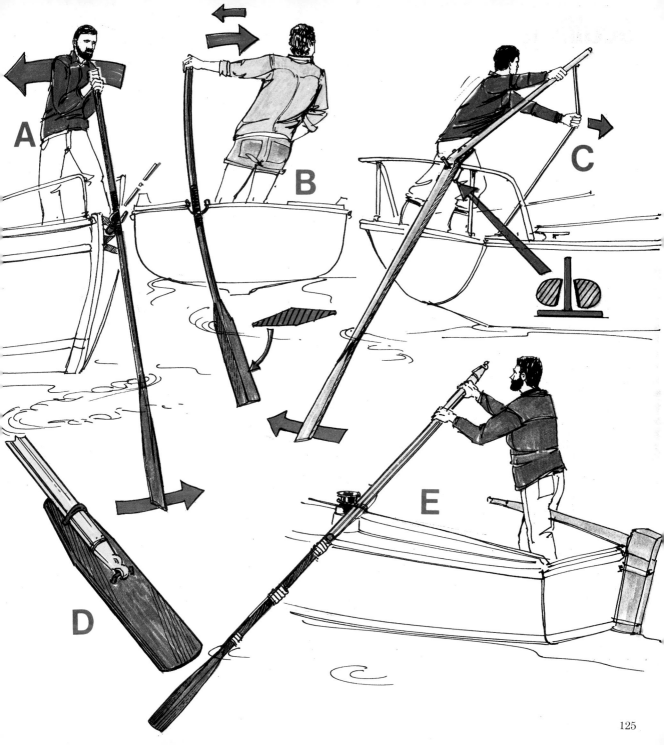

On tow

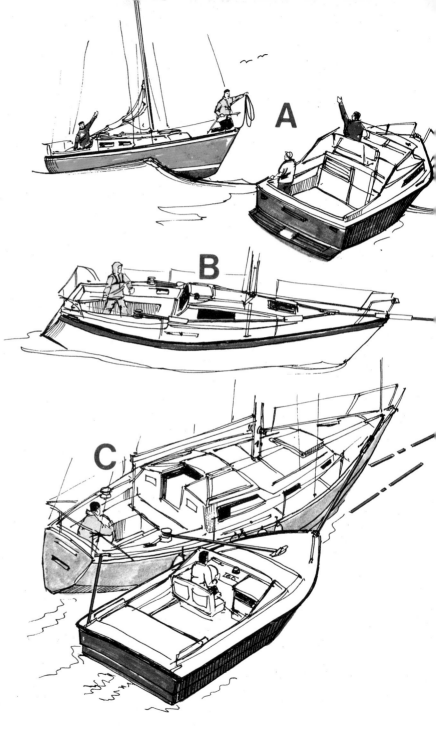

A. Having attracted attention, you can indicate your need for a tow by holding up a rope. It is safer by far to establish a firm understanding with the other skipper about any salvage fees that might be claimed. You should also agree to a system of simple hand signals — so, for example, you can slow him down, or make him change course, should the need arise.

B. That done, secure the tow-line round several strong points to spread the load — rather than relying on a single fitting — and guard against chafe. The rope must be made fast in such a way that it can be let go from either end and tied into the bow-fitting so it cannot jump out.

C. One of the best towing methods, particularly if you want to keep close control, is to make fast alongside. Here, the motorboat's spring warp is taking most of the load, while the fore and aft lines keep her angled slightly bows-in — an attitude which is commonly found most effective. It can also make steering less of a strain. Either way, the boat on tow can help by using her own rudder too.

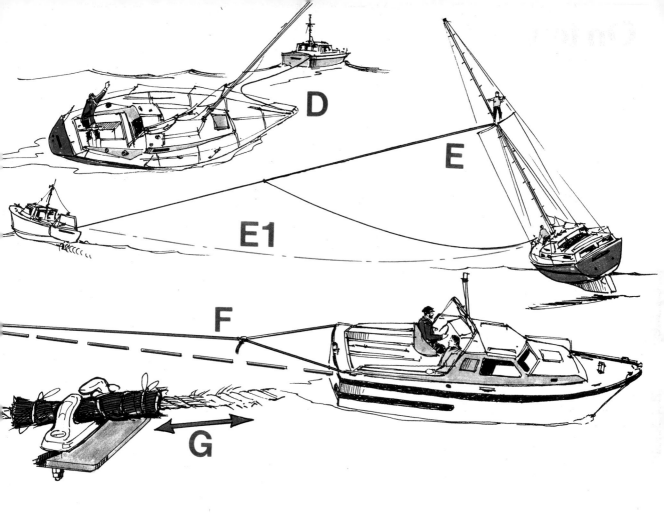

D. On a long tow, the rescue boat should take up the slack very gently, and move off in a straight line. If she goes too fast, the yacht can slew off course and become difficult to control, so it is best to take it easy.

E. The rescue boat can also help pull you clear of the shallows. In this example, a line on the bow bisects a warp made fast, at one end to the tow-boat, and at the other to the yacht's mast (suitable padded) at the shrouds. Once the yacht heels over, it reduces its draft and pulls clear, the crew (already positioned aloft) releases or cuts the warp, so the bow warp takes up the slack like a conventional tow-line.

E1. Or two lines can be used, transferring the load to the bow once she is clear.

F. If you're doing the towing, either make up a bridle to centralize the strain, or secure the line to the side that counteracts the paddle-wheel effect of your prop. Make fast to your strongest fittings and protect against chafe. And keep an eye on the line.

G. If it starts to get worn, you may have to ease it in or out, called 'freshening the nip'. Remember, towing involves very high loads, so extra care should be taken when handling and securing lines.

Towing with a dinghy

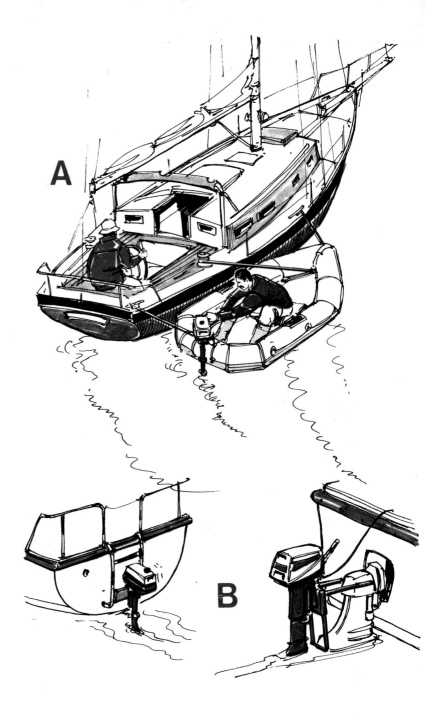

A. *The success of this particular manoeuvre depends largely on local conditions. In calm waters you can tow even large yachts with just a small amount of power, but when the sea gets up or the breeze begins to blow, the operation may be doomed to failure — and more trouble than it is worth. As always then, size up the situation in advance.*

B. *Given a little foresight of course, the drama can sometimes be avoided altogether. For example, a bracket on the mother ship could allow you to use the tender's outboard as auxiliary power, should the main engine fail. It can even be fitted to outdrive legs so you can use the main steering. But for our friends in the picture, such advice comes too late! As we saw earlier, a spring attached to sturdy fittings takes the main thrust, while fore and aft lines hold her slightly bows-in. Remember, while you can manoeuvre with the outboard in the normal way, the mother ship's steering can also be used to assist. And if you are the man in the dinghy, try to centralize your weight to stop her tipping up — and try to stay still.*

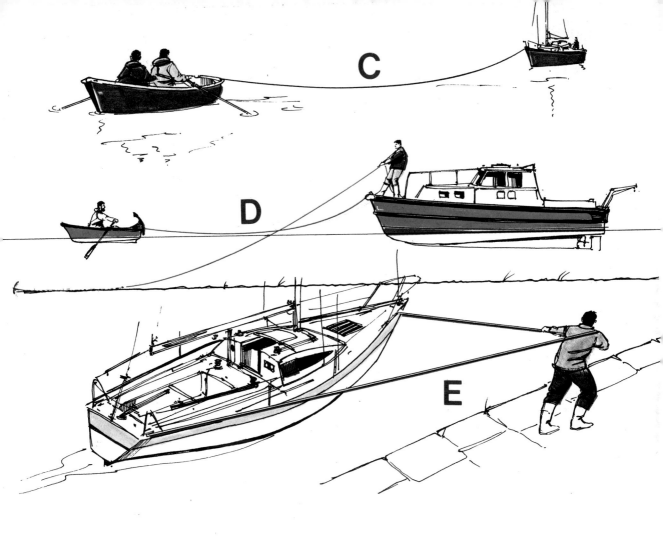

C. If you do not have an outboard you may find you can develop enough power by rowing. Try practising in fine weather. Some people actually enjoy it! But keep her on a fairly long line. If it is too short, it snatches and jerks.

D. You can also drag her along with anchors. Here, the skipper heaves in on one anchor cable, which propels the boat forward, while the man in the dinghy rows out ahead with another. As the first anchor is raised, the second is dropped — then the cycle begins again.

E. Finally, given a tow-path or quay, you can always 'bow-haul' your boat like this. Attach one end of the warp to the bow, and another to the stern, then loop it round your shoulders. To hold her off, and stop her rubbing along too close, keep the bow pointing out. That encourages her to 'swim' away from you — and for that reason makes it easier to keep her moving.

Fouled anchor

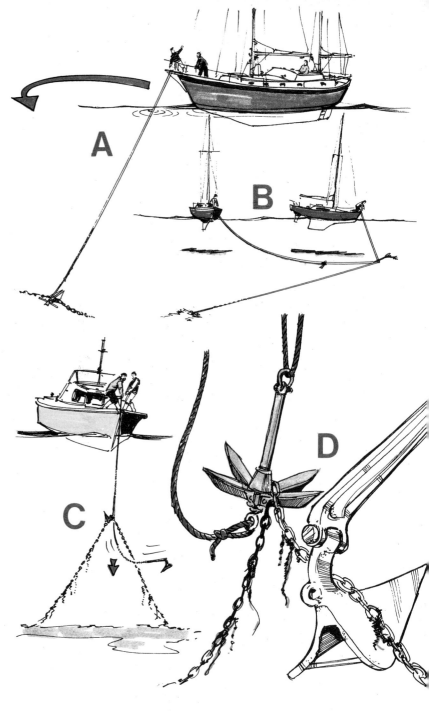

There is no certain, 'text book', or guaranteed method of dislodging an anchor that's trapped — so experiment!

A. Try motoring over the top of it with the anchor cable taut. Try going round in circles, so the pull comes from a different direction. Try the same tactics with the anchor cable slack. But keep trying!

B. If the cable itself gets caught, let out more scope, then motor round in circles. Naturally, it pays to work out in advance whether you should circle to the left or to the right, but in any case, you'll soon find out. If you get it wrong, the cable will tighten. In extreme cases the cable may warp itself round the obstacle several times as the boat swings on the tide, and will prove even more of a challenge . . .

C. If the anchor can be lifted, but still remains hooked, haul up tight, then quickly let go. With any luck it should swing itself clear.

D. Another possible solution is to hook the obstruction with another, smaller anchor. In the example a grapnel has been lowered on a slip line and hooked round the chain. It is then pulled tight, to free the main anchor which would then be raised to the surface. To release the grapnel, haul on the tripping line and let the slip run free.

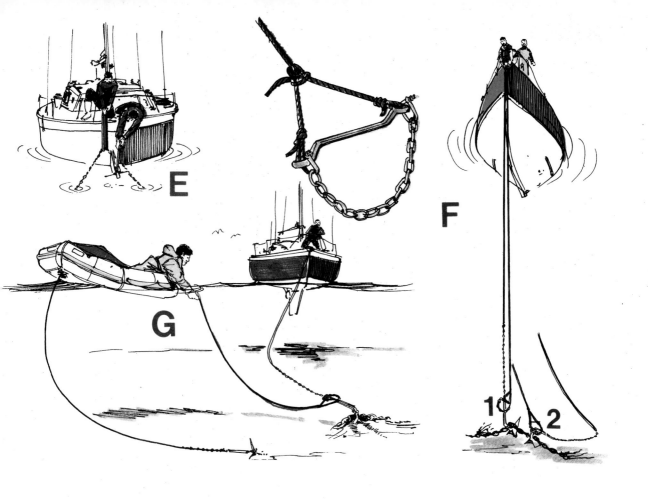

E. But perhaps you can get the offending chain close to the surface? If so, you may be able to pull it clear with a slip line while your crew frees the anchor itself . . .

F. A more ingenious answer is an impromptu tripping line. You could make it from various odds and ends, though in the example, its main components are a ring spanner, a length of chain, and a couple of shackles. Attached to a bridle, then lowered down the tight anchor cable, it may be persuaded far enough over the shank to allow you to jerk it clear.

G. Sometimes, this particular 'trick' is more effective from the dinghy — which should itself be anchored to prevent unnecessary movement. But what if none of that works? The final option is to cast the cable free attached to a buoy — which, incidentally, should be well proportioned, as chain is surprisingly heavy.

Aground

Different boats behave in different ways when they strike the bottom under sail. For example, a fin keeler

A. heeled over on a beat at the moment of impact, will stop, then come slowly upright, increasing the draft, which in turn, makes the keel dig in. On the other hand, when a twin keeler

B. 'bottoms' and ceases to heel, her draft will usually decrease, so she floats clear, giving you time to react, and with luck, sail into deeper water. But if you do find yourself stuck it is essential to try and get off at once — particulaly on a falling tide.

C. So, having sailed a fin keeler aground, to windward, try backing the jib. It can sheer the bow roud while at the same time keeping the boat heeled, and the draft at a minimum.

D. If you sail aground on the run, gybe round instantly, using whatever momentum you have, plus the effect of the boom swinging over, to induce heel, and drive her round. If none of that works, you may have to lay a kedge — without delay. But first, work, out where the direction of pull can do the most good.

E. With a short-keeled boat, you may be able to pull the bows round (with help from the engine) as she pivots on the forward edge of the fin.

F. A long keeled boat, in contrast, can cut a trench in the mud which will hold her sideways, and for that reason may be easier to coax out 'backwards' with a line from the after-deck, and the engine in astern. If she has a cutaway forefoot, get as much weight at the bow as possible, to reduce the deeper draft aft.

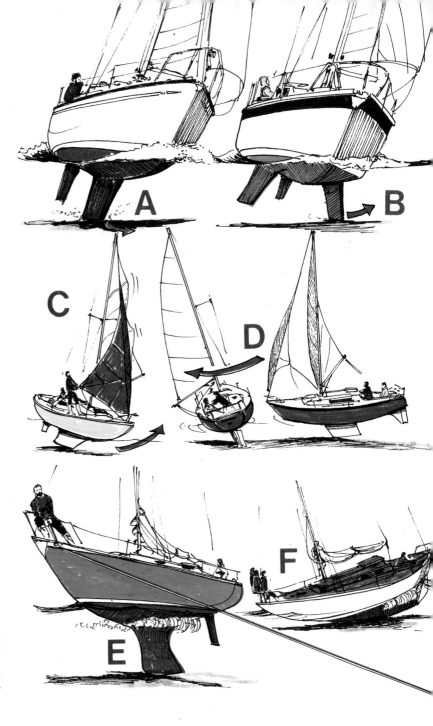

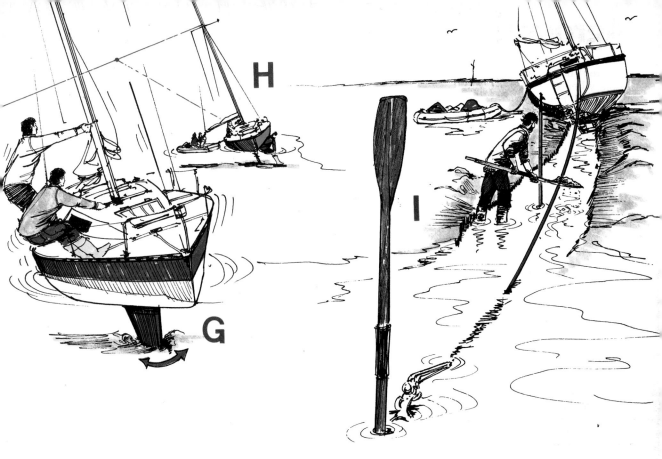

G. If your boat is light, you may be able to rock her from side to side, just by using your weight, and in that way, 'wriggle' her clear. But you will still need to keep her moving, or pointing, in the right direction, either under sail, or with help from the engine. Sometimes you can free her just by leaning out and heeling her over, to reduce the draft. On other occasions, something more drastic may be called for.

H. A kedge with the warp attached to the mast high up, at the hounds, which then acts as a lever, may do the trick. The effect can be enhanced by attaching additional tensioning lines to the anchor warp, and leading them back to the deck through blocks. But you should make sure that everything's strong enough. Kedging out on the end of the spinnaker halyard, for instance, may cause stresses and strains which the relevant sheaves and blocks were never designed to take.

To help her heel, and reduce weight and therefore draft, it may be necessary to get the crew off into the dinghy, along with some of the gear. From that position, they might push down on the end if the boom which will help.

In shoal (and warm?) waters, and given a small enough boat, hardy skippers slip over the side, get their backs under the bow, and push with the feet . .

I. But if at the end of the day, you are still stuck and the tide goes out, you may just have to make the best of it. If you have enough energy left, dig a trench with whatever tools you can find, to provide a line of escape. Having done that, it's a good idea to mark the 'ditch' — with an oar and boathook perhaps — so you know which direction you should aim for when the water comes back. Again, lighten the vessel by getting as much weight as possible into the dinghy.

133

Make it easy for yourself

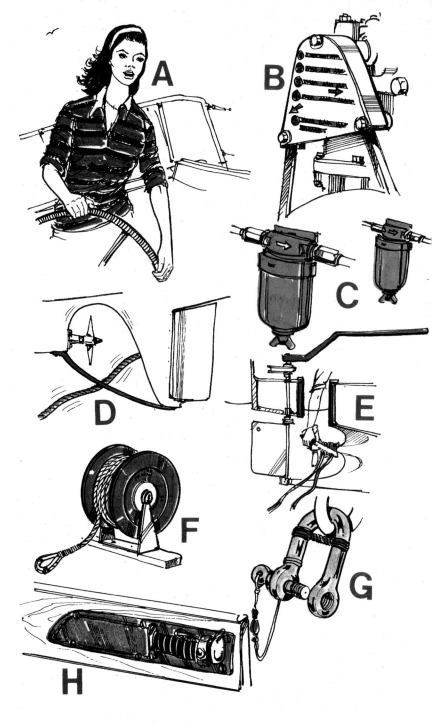

A. If everyone knows how to handle the boat, it frees you to sort out any sudden emergency.

B. In the same way, labelling all the relevant engine instructions, in the motor itself, can save time and jog memories — yours perhaps?

C. If possible, fit large filters and water separators etc in the fuel lines, preferably with a switch-over facility, so you can change to clean fuel while you deal with the blockage.

D. Is your prop unprotected? A simple strap will help keep out warps, bags, and nets . . .

E. At the design stage you might be able to work in 'lifeboat-style' access hatches so you can get to the prop. Even easier, is a hole through the rudder, which makes it possible to rig emergency steering lines. Similarly, an auxiliary tiller provides back-up should the steering cables fail.

F. Ropes are less likely to tangle if you keep them on drums. Eyes on the end make them easier to fasten.

G. When the wind blows and waves roll, fingers begin to fumble, so 'mouse' any shackles for special tasks by tying them on like this. And if you do not already have captive shackle pins, drill the ends and secure them with lanyards — ideally with small fishing swivels to stop the line getting tangled.

H. Where is the knife? Essential emergency equipment should be kept in a special place known to all on board, and instantly ready for use. Also every member of a crew should also carry a knife.

Crew and rope (11)

A good crew works in harmony with the skipper, offering advice and asking questions from time to time, but obeying instructions when necessary. In a sudden emergency, for example, it is often essential to avoid prolonged discussion, and let the skipper take overall control. Even if you are married to him!

At the same time, the crew should develop basic skills, and know how to make fast, to fend off, and to get ashore safely. Of course, a basic knowledge of knots and hitches is fundamental, both to good crewmanship and seamanship in general. In practice, the actual number of knots needed are few; the skill comes in applying simple techniques to different situations.

To start from first principles, you should know how to make fast to all kinds of fittings, with knots or hitches which remain secure, yet are easy to release.

You should also realise that sometimes, the first priority is simply to take the strain. Once ashore with the warps, you should wind a turn of rope round a bollard or cleat, and let the craft take up the slack before making fast with a knot.

On the other hand, when getting underway for example, the emphasis might be on ease of release; making loops which slip free at a moment's notice.

By the same token, are your warps neatly stowed, yet readily accessible, or are they jumbled and twisted?

Competent crews, like skippers, should always be alert to the uniqueness of each situation.

Crewing and seamanship

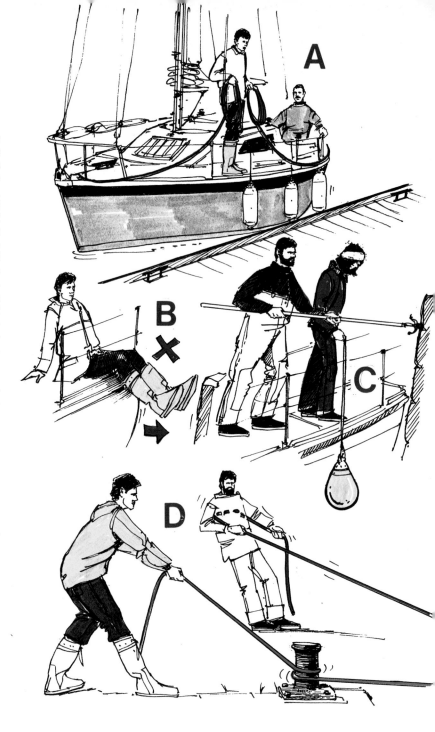

A. When coming alongside, it is often easiest to step ashore from the widest part of the boat. But check with the skipper first. He may be planning a different approach. Assuming all is well, be prepared with bow and stern lines led round the outside of stanchions, lifelines and fenders. Hold them in loose coils which 'unwind' easily. And brace yourself — against the shrouds perhaps. For added security, some people stand with one foot inboard, and one on the outboard side of the guard rails. But however you wedge yourself in, wait patiently, and do not try and jump across the gap. If the skipper stops too short, it is wiser to have him go round again, than to risk falling overboard between the boat and the dock.

B. Never fend off with your feet. Even a small boat's momentum takes some stopping, and damaged topsides are better than broken legs! So fend off with less valuable things . . .

C. . . . like a boathook. But remember, a sudden impact can still hurt you, so hold it to one side of your body. Alternatively, have a large dumpy fender handy, and drop it in where you see the boat is most vulnerable.

D. When you finally get ashore, take a turn round a bollard or cleat and let friction hold the boat until she's safely at rest. If you do have to take the strain, feed the warp round your back 'mountaineer style' using body weight and friction to hold her.

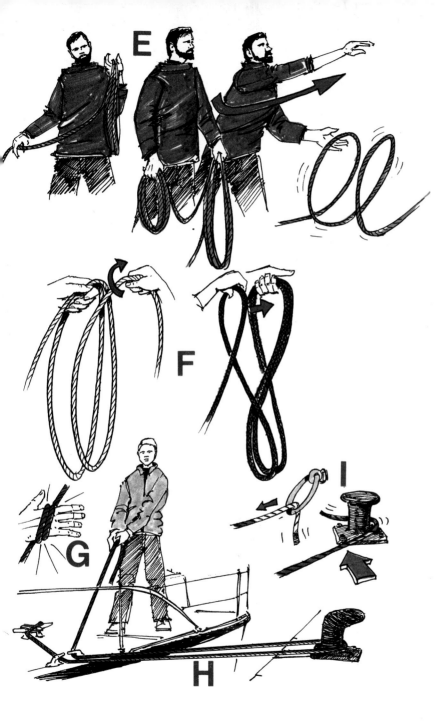

E. You may have to throw a line ashore, in which case it is advisable to make two coils, one smaller and tighter than the other so it is easier to throw. With a broad sweep, cast it high and clear, releasing the larger coil as you do so.

F. Different cordage should be coiled in different ways. Laid ropes need a twist to make them lie flat; plaited ropes hang together best when made into 'figures of eight'.

G. Never take a turn round your hand. A sudden pull may crush your fingers!

H. Mooring lines can be re-rigged as loops or 'slip warps' to enable you to cast-off from on board. Although, if any load is to be taken, it is better to take a turn round a cleat. And remember not to lay to them for too long, as any chafe in the middle of the warp can ruin it.

I. If you use a ring, feed the warp from underneath so the line cannot jam. When using a bollard, it is worth making sure that the tail is to leeward. Otherwise, in high winds, it can flip over and bind at the last moment.

What Knots to use

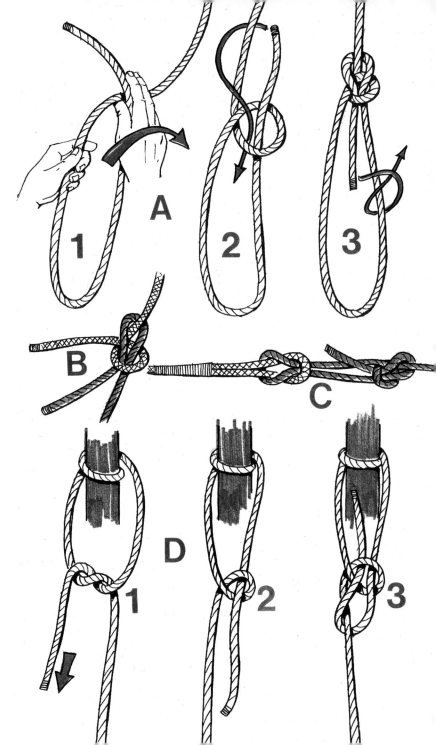

The bowline is a knot for forming a loop (or eye) in the end of a line. There are numerous ways of tying it, but this method is one of the simplest:

A1. Start with a loop, then twist the right hand to form a small loop . . .

A2. . . . feed the tail round the back of the standing part . . .

A3. . . . and back down the small loop again. Like mountaineers, for added security you can finish off with a half-hitch. It is a particularly useful safety measure with springy synthetic rope.

B. The same bowline 'movement' can be used for quickly joining two lines together . . .

C. . . . or joining a line to an eye. But first make a loop that 'interlocks'. It is kinder to both lines.

D1. When making fast to a post, you can start with a round turn, then follow up with a bowline. But remember you will be tying it 'back to front', or the wrong way round. Wrap the tail once round the standing part . . .

D2. . . . then pull on it. Now it is in a loop.

D3. Feed it round the end nearest you and back down the loop again.

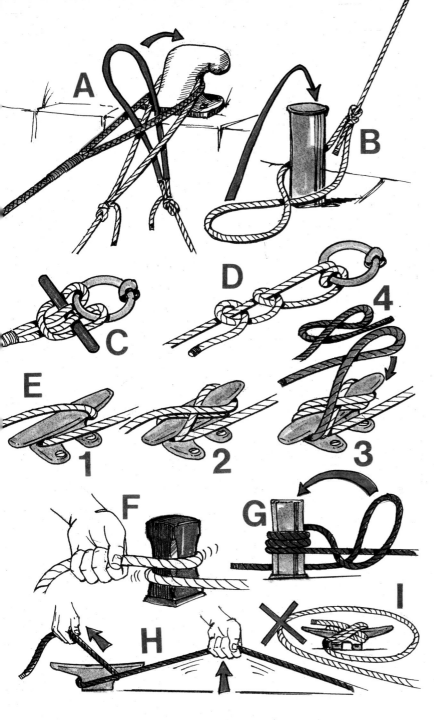

A. When dropping a line on a bollard, feed it through your neighbours' loops — then everyone can release their warps without disturbing the others. Make sure your loop is large enough to allow other warps to pass through it. A plastic tube will protect it from chafe.

B. If you are worried about an upward pull on a post, twist another loop on top to hold it.

C. A short bar or piece of wood makes it easy to fix an 'eye' to a ring, and it can be released under load.

D. Alternatively, make a round turn, which takes the load, and lock it with two half hitches. It is easier to let go under tension than a bowline.

E. To make fast to a cleat, take the line round the back of the cleat (1) and add friction with figures of eights (2). Finish off, if necessary, with a twist to lock it (3). If you wish, the twist can be made with a loop (4) so it releases with a short sharp tug.

F. You can wrap a line round a samson post or bollard so it takes up the load, then ease or 'surge' it to let out more slack . . .

G. . . . but if you want to make fast, add more turns for friction, and drop a loop like this over the top. It is particularly useful when dealing with anchor chain on the foredeck, and can also be released under load. Never use a clove hitch in such circumstances, as it can jam.

H. One way of tightening a line is to pull it out or up, while 'grabbing the slack gained round a cleat. Often called 'swigging'.

I. But never take up the slack on a mooring warp by winding the standing part round the cleat. It locks everything solid!

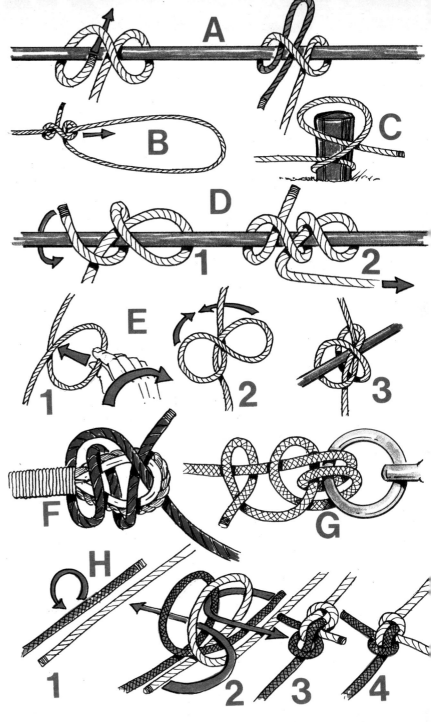

A. The clove hitch *is ideal for attaching fenders to lifelines, and can be finished off with a loop, so it is easy to undo . . .*

B. *. . . you can make it round itself to form a quick 'noose'*

C. *. . . . or drop it over a post, but only when no heavy strain is expected, as it is hard to release.*

D. A rolling hitch, *for making up to ropes or spars, is like a clove hitch with an extra turn, and resists loads at an angle. Ideal for taking the strain off another rope. Use it for a flag halyard on the shroud.*

E. The constrictor knot *can either be formed by 'twisting' and 'pushing', or made similar to a clove hitch. It grips rounded objects extremely tightly when put under load, and is difficult to let go.*

F. The becket hitch *is a quick and easy way of making fast to a rope with an eye in it.*

G. The fisherman's bend *locks up even tighter than a round turn and two half hitches, and for that reason is often used on anchor lines.*

H. Hunter's bend *is a quick and highly efficient way of joining two lines, especially for slippery synthetic ones. First, hold both ends together and then twist them to form the loop. Pass the ends through as shown.*

INDEX